DAN-25   DANTES SUBJECT STANDARDIZED TESTS (DSST)

This is your
PASSBOOK for...

Introduction to Law Enforcement

Test Preparation Study Guide
Questions & Answers

COPYRIGHT NOTICE

This book is SOLELY intended for, is sold ONLY to, and its use is RESTRICTED to individual, bona fide applicants or candidates who qualify by virtue of having seriously filed applications for appropriate license, certificate, professional and/or promotional advancement, higher school matriculation, scholarship, or other legitimate requirements of education and/or governmental authorities.

This book is NOT intended for use, class instruction, tutoring, training, duplication, copying, reprinting, excerption, or adaptation, etc., by:

1) Other publishers
2) Proprietors and/or Instructors of "Coaching" and/or Preparatory Courses
3) Personnel and/or Training Divisions of commercial, industrial, and governmental organizations
4) Schools, colleges, or universities and/or their departments and staffs, including teachers and other personnel
5) Testing Agencies or Bureaus
6) Study groups which seek by the purchase of a single volume to copy and/or duplicate and/or adapt this material for use by the group as a whole without having purchased individual volumes for each of the members of the group
7) Et al.

Such persons would be in violation of appropriate Federal and State statutes.

PROVISION OF LICENSING AGREEMENTS – Recognized educational, commercial, industrial, and governmental institutions and organizations, and others legitimately engaged in educational pursuits, including training, testing, and measurement activities, may address request for a licensing agreement to the copyright owners, who will determine whether, and under what conditions, including fees and charges, the materials in this book may be used them. In other words, a licensing facility exists for the legitimate use of the material in this book on other than an individual basis. However, it is asseverated and affirmed here that the material in this book CANNOT be used without the receipt of the express permission of such a licensing agreement from the Publishers. Inquiries re licensing should be addressed to the company, attention rights and permissions department.

All rights reserved, including the right of reproduction in whole or in part, in any form or by any means, electronic or mechanical, including photocopying, recording, or by any information storage and retrieval system, without permission in writing from the Publisher.

Copyright © 2025 by
National Learning Corporation

212 Michael Drive, Syosset, NY 11791
(516) 921-8888 • www.passbooks.com
E-mail: info@passbooks.com

PASSBOOK® SERIES

THE *PASSBOOK® SERIES* has been created to prepare applicants and candidates for the ultimate academic battlefield – the examination room.

At some time in our lives, each and every one of us may be required to take an examination – for validation, matriculation, admission, qualification, registration, certification, or licensure.

Based on the assumption that every applicant or candidate has met the basic formal educational standards, has taken the required number of courses, and read the necessary texts, the *PASSBOOK® SERIES* furnishes the one special preparation which may assure passing with confidence, instead of failing with insecurity. Examination questions – together with answers – are furnished as the basic vehicle for study so that the mysteries of the examination and its compounding difficulties may be eliminated or diminished by a sure method.

This book is meant to help you pass your examination provided that you qualify and are serious in your objective.

The entire field is reviewed through the huge store of content information which is succinctly presented through a provocative and challenging approach – the question-and-answer method.

A climate of success is established by furnishing the correct answers at the end of each test.

You soon learn to recognize types of questions, forms of questions, and patterns of questioning. You may even begin to anticipate expected outcomes.

You perceive that many questions are repeated or adapted so that you can gain acute insights, which may enable you to score many sure points.

You learn how to confront new questions, or types of questions, and to attack them confidently and work out the correct answers.

You note objectives and emphases, and recognize pitfalls and dangers, so that you may make positive educational adjustments.

Moreover, you are kept fully informed in relation to new concepts, methods, practices, and directions in the field.

You discover that you are actually taking the examination all the time: you are preparing for the examination by "taking" an examination, not by reading extraneous and/or supererogatory textbooks.

In short, this PASSBOOK®, used directedly, should be an important factor in helping you to pass your test.

NONTRADITIONAL EDUCATION

Students returning to school as adults bring more varied experience to their studies than do the teenagers who begin college shortly after graduating from high school. As a result, there are numerous programs for students with nontraditional learning curves. Hundreds of colleges and universities grant degrees to people who cannot attend classes at a regular campus or have already learned what the college is supposed to teach.

You can earn nontraditional education credits in many ways:
- Passing standardized exams
- Demonstrating knowledge gained through experience
- Completing campus-based coursework, and
- Taking courses off campus

Some methods of assessing learning for credit are objective, such as standardized tests. Others are more subjective, such as a review of life experiences.

With some help from four hypothetical characters – Alice, Vin, Lynette, and Jorge – this article describes nontraditional ways of earning educational credit. It begins by describing programs in which you can earn a high school diploma without spending 4 years in a classroom. The college picture is more complicated, so it is presented in two parts: one on gaining credit for what you know through course work or experience, and a second on college degree programs. The final section lists resources for locating more information.

Earning High School Credit

People who were prevented from finishing high school as teenagers have several options if they want to do so as adults. Some major cities have back-to-school programs that allow adults to attend high school classes with current students. But the more practical alternatives for most adults are to take the General Educational Development (GED) tests or to earn a high school diploma by demonstrating their skills or taking correspondence classes.

Of course, these options do not match the experience of staying in high school and graduating with one's friends. But they are viable alternatives for adult learners committed to meeting and, often, continuing their educational goals.

GED Program

Alice quit high school her sophomore year and took a job to help support herself, her younger brother, and their newly widowed mother. Now an adult, she wants to earn her high school diploma – and then go on to college. Because her job as head cook and her family responsibilities keep her busy during the day, she plans to get a high school equivalency diploma. She will study for, and take, the GED tests. Every year, about half a million adults earn their high school credentials this way. A GED diploma is accepted in lieu of a high school one by more than 90 percent of employers, colleges, and universities, so it is a good choice for someone like Alice.

The GED testing program is sponsored by the American Council on Education and State and local education departments. It consists of examinations in five subject areas: Writing, science, mathematics, social studies, and literature and the arts. The tests also measure skills such as analytical ability, problem solving, reading comprehension, and ability to understand and apply information. Most of the questions are multiple choice; the writing test includes an essay section on a topic of general interest.

Eligibility rules for taking the exams vary, but some states require that you must be at least 18. Tests are given in English, Spanish, and French. In addition to standard print, versions in large print, Braille, and audiocassette are also available. Total time allotted for the tests is 7 1/2 hours.

The GED tests are not easy. About one-fourth of those who complete the exams every year do not pass. Passing scores are established by administering the tests to a sample of graduating high school seniors. The minimum standard score is set so that about one-third of graduating seniors would not pass the tests if they took them.

Because of the difficulty of the tests, people need to prepare themselves to take them. Often, they start by taking the Official GED Practice Tests, usually available through a local adult education center. Centers are listed in your phone book's blue pages under "Adult Education," "Continuing Education," or "GED." Adult education centers also have information about GED preparation classes and self-study materials. Classes are generally arranged to accommodate adults' work schedules. National Learning Corporation publishes several study guides that aim to thoroughly prepare test-takers for the GED.

School districts, colleges, adult education centers, and community organizations have information about GED testing schedules and practice tests. For more information, contact them, your nearest GED testing center, or:

GED Testing Service
One Dupont Circle, NW, Suite 250
Washington, DC 20036-1163
1(800) 62-MY GED (626-9433)
(202) 939-9490

Skills Demonstration

Adults who have acquired high school level skills through experience might be eligible for the National External Diploma Program. This alternative to the GED does not involve any direct instruction. Instead, adults seeking a high school diploma must demonstrate mastery of 65 competencies in 8 general areas: Communication; computation; occupational preparedness; and self, social, consumer, scientific, and technological awareness.

Mastery is shown through the completion of the tasks. For example, a participant could prove competency in computation by measuring a room for carpeting, figuring out the amount of carpet needed, and computing the cost.

Before being accepted for the program, adults undergo an evaluation. Tests taken at one of the program's offices measure reading, writing, and mathematics abilities. A take-home segment includes a self-assessment of current skills, an individual skill evaluation, and an occupational interest and aptitude test.

Adults accepted for the program have weekly meetings with an assessor. At the meeting, the assessor reviews the participant's work from the previous week. If the task has not been completed properly, the assessor explains the mistake. Participants continue to correct their errors until they master each competency. A high school diploma is awarded upon proven mastery of all 65 competencies.

Fourteen States and the District of Columbia now offer the External Diploma Program. For more information, contact:

External Diploma Program
One Dupont Circle, NW, Suite 250
Washington, DC 20036-1193
(202) 939-9475

Correspondence and Distance Study

Vin dropped out of high school during his junior year because his family's frequent moves made it difficult for him to continue his studies. He promised himself at the time he dropped out that he would someday finish the courses needed for his diploma. For people like Vin, who prefer to earn a traditional diploma in a nontraditional way, there are about a dozen accredited courses of study for earning a high school diploma by correspondence, or distance study. The programs are either privately run, affiliated with a university, or administered by a State education department.

Distance study diploma programs have no residency requirements, allowing students to continue their studies from almost any location. Depending on the course of study, students need not be enrolled full time and usually have more flexible schedules for finishing their work. Selection of courses ranges from vo-tech to college prep, and some programs place different emphasis on the types of diplomas offered. University affiliated schools, for example, allow qualified students to take college courses along with their high school ones. Students can then apply the college credits toward a degree at that university or transfer them to another institution.

Taking courses by distance study is often more challenging and time consuming than attending classes, especially for adults who have other obligations. Success depends on each student's motivation. Students usually do reading assignments on their own. Written exercises, which they complete and send to an instructor for grading, supplement their reading material.

A list of some accredited high schools that offer diplomas by distance study is available free from the Distance Education and Training Council, formerly known as the National Home Study Council. Request the "DETC Directory of Accredited Institutions" from:

The Distance Education and Training Council
1601 18th Street, NW.
Washington, DC 20009-2529
(202) 234-5100

Some publications profiling nontraditional college programs include addresses and descriptions of several high school correspondence ones. See the Resources section at the end of this article for more information.

Getting College Credit For What You Know

Adults can receive college credit for prior coursework, by passing examinations, and documenting experiential learning. With help from a college advisor, nontraditional students should assess their skills, establish their educational goals, and determine the number of college credits they might be eligible for.

Even before you meet with a college advisor, you should collect all your school and training records. Then, make a list of all knowledge and abilities acquired through experience, no matter how irrelevant they seem to your chosen field. Next, determine your educational goals: What specific field do you wish to study? What kind of a degree do you want? Finally, determine how your past work fits into the field of study. Later on, you will evaluate educational programs to find one that's right for you.

People who have complex educational or experiential learning histories might want to have their learning evaluated by the Regents Credit Bank. The Credit Bank, operated by Regents College of the University of the State of New York, allows people to consolidate credits earned through college, experience, or other methods. Special assessments are available for Regents College enrollees whose knowledge in a specific field cannot be adequately evaluated by standardized exams. For more information, contact the Regents Credit Bank at:

Regents College
7 Columbia Circle
Albany, NY 12203-5159
(518) 464-8500

Credit For Prior College Coursework

When Lynette was in college during the 1970s, she attended several different schools and took a variety of courses. She did well in some classes and poorly in others. Now that she is a successful business owner and has more focus, Lynette thinks she should forget about her previous coursework and start from scratch. Instead, she should start from where she is.

Lynette should have all her transcripts sent to the colleges or universities of her choice and let an admissions officer determine which classes are applicable toward a degree. A few credits here and there may not seem like much, but they add up. Even if the subjects do not seem relevant to any major, they might be counted as elective credits toward a degree. And comparing the cost of transcripts with the cost of college courses, it makes sense to spend a few dollars per transcript for a chance to save hundreds, and perhaps thousands, of dollars in books and tuition.

Rules for transferring credits apply to all prior coursework at accredited colleges and universities, whether done on campus or off. Courses completed off campus, often called extended learning, include those available to students through independent study and correspondence. Many schools have extended learning programs; Brigham Young University, for example, offers more than 300 courses through its Department of Independent Study. One type of extended learning is distance learning, a form of correspondence study by technological means such as television, video and audio, CD-ROM, electronic mail, and computer tutorials. See the Resources section at the end of this article for more information about publications available from the National University Continuing Education Association.

Any previously earned college credits should be considered for transfer, no matter what the subject or the grade received. Many schools do not accept the transfer of courses graded below a C or ones taken more than a designated number of years ago. Some colleges and universities also have limits on the number of credits that can be transferred and applied toward a degree. But not all do. For example, Thomas Edison State College, New Jersey's State college for adults, accepts the transfer of all 120 hours of credit required for a baccalaureate degree – provided all the credits are transferred from regionally accredited schools, no more than 80 are at the junior college level, and the student's grades overall and in the field of study average out to C.

To assign credit for prior coursework, most schools require original transcripts. This means you must complete a form or send a written, signed request to have your transcripts released directly to a college or university. Once you have chosen the schools you want to apply to, contact the schools you attended before. Find out how much each transcript costs, and ask them to send your transcripts to the ones you are applying to. Write a letter that includes your name (and names used during attendance, if different) and dates of attendance, along with the names and addresses of the schools to which your transcripts should be sent. Include payment and mail to the registrar at the schools you have attended. The registrar's office will process your request and send an official transcript of your coursework to the colleges or universities you have designated.

Credit For Noncollege Courses

Colleges and universities are not the only ones that offer classes. Volunteer organizations and employers often provide formal training worth college credit. The American Council on Education has two programs that assess thousands of specific courses and make recommendations on the amount of college credit they are worth. Colleges and universities accept the recommendations or use them as guidelines.

One program evaluates educational courses sponsored by government agencies, business and industry, labor unions, and professional and voluntary organizations. It is the Program on Noncollegiate Sponsored Instruction (PONSI). Some of the training seminars Alice has participated in covered topics such as food preparation, kitchen safety, and nutrition. Although she has not yet earned her GED, Alice can earn college credit because of her completion of these formal job-training seminars. The number of credits each seminar is worth does not hinge on Alice's current eligibility for college enrollment.

The other program evaluates courses offered by the Army, Navy, Air Force, Marines, Coast Guard, and Department of Defense. It is the Military Evaluations Program. Jorge has never attended college, but the engineering technology classes he completed as part of his military training are worth college credit. And as an Army veteran, Jorge is eligible for a service that takes the evaluations one step further. The Army/American Council on Education Registry Transcript System (AARTS) will provide Jorge with an individualized transcript of American Council on Education credit recommendations for all courses he completed, the military occupational specialties (MOS's) he held, and examinations he passed while in the Army. All Army and National Guard enlisted personnel and veterans who enlisted after October 1981 are eligible for the transcript. Similar services are being considered by the Navy and Marine Corps.

To obtain a free transcript, see your Army Education Center for a 5454R transcript request form. Include your name, Social Security number, basic active service date, and complete address where you want the transcript sent. Mail your request to:
AARTS Operations Center
415 McPherson Ave.
Fort Leavenworth, KS 66027-1373

Recommendations for PONSI are published in *The National Guide to Educational Credit for Training Programs;* military program recommendations are in *The Guide to the Evaluation of Educational Experiences in the Armed Forces.* See the Resources section at the end of this article for more information about these publications.

Former military personnel who took a foreign language course through the Defense Language Institute may request course transcripts by sending their name, Social Security number, course title, duration of the course, and graduation date to:

Commandant, Defense Language Institute
Attn: ATFL-DAA-AR
Transcripts
Presidio of Monterey
Monterey, CA 93944-5006

Not all of Jorge's and Alice's courses have been assessed by the American Council on Education. Training courses that have no Council credit recommendation should still be assessed by an advisor at the schools they want to attend. Course descriptions, class notes, test scores, and other documentation may be helpful for comparing training courses to their college equivalents. An oral examination or other demonstration of competency might also be required.

There is no guarantee you will receive all the credits you are seeking – but you certainly won't if you make no attempt.

Credit By Examination

Standardized tests are the best-known method of receiving college credit without taking courses. These exams are often taken by high school students seeking advanced placement for college, but they are also available to adult learners. Testing programs and colleges and universities offer exams in a number of subjects. Two U.S. Government institutes have foreign language exams for employees that also may be worth college credit.

It is important to understand that receiving a passing score on these exams does not mean you get college credit automatically. Each school determines which test results it will accept, minimum scores required, how scores are converted for credit, and the amount of credit, if any, to be assigned. Most colleges and universities accept the American Council on Education credit recommendations, published every other year in the 250-page *Guide to Educational Credit by Examination*. For more information, contact:

The American Council on Education
Credit by Examination Program
One Dupont Circle, Suite 250
Washington, DC 20036-1193
(202) 939-9434

Testing programs:

You might know some of the five national testing programs by their acronyms or initials: CLEP, ACT PEP: RCE, DANTES, AP, and NOCTI. (The meanings of these initialisms are explained below.) There is some overlap among programs; for example, four of them have introductory accounting exams. Since you will not be awarded credit more than once for a specific subject, you should carefully evaluate each program for the subject exams you wish to take. And before taking an exam, make sure you will be awarded credit by the college or university you plan to attend.

CLEP (College-Level Examination Program), administered by the College Board, is the most widely accepted of the national testing programs; more than 2,800 accredited schools award credit for passing exam scores. Each test covers material taught in basic undergraduate courses. There are five general exams – English composition, humanities, college mathematics, natural sciences, and social sciences and history – and many subject exams. Most exams are entirely multiple-choice, but English composition exams may include an essay section. For more information, contact:

    CLEP
    P.O. Box 6600
    Princeton, NJ 08541-6600
    (609) 771-7865

ACT PEP: RCE (American College Testing Proficiency Exam Program: Regents College Examinations) tests are given in 38 subjects within arts and sciences, business, education, and nursing. Each exam is recommended for either lower- or upper-level credit. Exams contain either objective or extended response questions, and are graded according to a standard score, letter grade, or pass/fail. Fees vary, depending on the subject and type of exam. For more information or to request free study guides, contact:

    ACT PEP: Regents College Examinations
    P.O. Box 4014
    Iowa City, IA 52243
    (319) 337-1387
    (New York State residents must contact Regents College directly.)

DANTES (Defense Activity for Nontraditional Education Support) standardized tests are developed by the Educational Testing Service for the Department of Defense. Originally administered only to military personnel, the exams have been available to the public since 1983. About 50 subject tests cover business, mathematics, social science, physical science, humanities, foreign languages, and applied technology. Most of the tests consist entirely of multiple-choice questions. Schools determine their own administering fees and testing schedules. For more information or to request free study sheets, contact:

    DANTES Program Office
    Mail Stop 31-X
    Educational Testing Service
    Princeton, NJ 08541
    1(800) 257-9484

The AP (Advanced Placement) Program is a cooperative effort between secondary schools and colleges and universities. AP exams are developed each year by committees of college and high school faculty appointed by the College Board and assisted by consultants from the Educational Testing Service. Subjects include arts and languages, natural sciences, computer science, social sciences, history, and mathematics. Most tests are 2 or 3 hours long and include both multiple-choice and essay questions. AP courses are available to help students prepare for exams, which are offered in the spring. For more information about the Advanced Placement Program, contact:

    Advanced Placement Services
    P.O. Box 6671
    Princeton, NJ 08541-6671
    (609) 771-7300

NOCTI (National Occupational Competency Testing Institute) assessments are designed for people like Alice, who have vocational-technical skills that cannot be evaluated by other tests. NOCTI assesses competency at two levels: Student/job ready and teacher/experienced worker. Standardized evaluations are available for occupations such as auto-body repair, electronics, mechanical drafting, quantity food preparation, and upholstering. The tests consist of multiple-choice questions and a performance component. Other services include workshops, customized assessments, and pre-testing. For more information, contact:

NOCTI
500 N. Bronson Ave.
Ferris State University
Big Rapids, MI 49307
(616) 796-4699

Colleges and universities:

Many colleges and universities have credit-by-exam programs, through which students earn credit by passing a comprehensive exam for a course offered by the institution. Among the most widely recognized are the programs at Ohio University, the University of North Carolina, Thomas Edison State College, and New York University.

Ohio University offers about 150 examinations for credit. In addition, you may sometimes arrange to take special examinations in non-laboratory courses offered at Ohio University. To take a test for credit, you must enroll in the course. If you plan to transfer the credit earned, you also need written permission from an official at your school. Books and study materials are available, for a cost, through the university. Exams must be taken within 6 months of the enrollment date; most last 3 hours. You may arrange to take the exam off campus if you do not live near the university.

Ohio University is on the quarter-hour system; most courses are worth 4 quarter hours, the equivalent of 3 semester hours. For more information, contact:

Independent Study
Tupper Hall 302
Ohio University
Athens, OH 45701-2979
1(800) 444-2910
(614) 593-2910

The University of North Carolina offers a credit-by-examination option for 140 independent study (correspondence) courses in foreign languages, humanities, social sciences, mathematics, business administration, education, electrical and computer engineering, health administration, and natural sciences. To take an exam, you must request and receive approval from both the course instructor and the independent studies department. Exams must be taken within six months of enrollment, and you may register for no more than two at a time. If you are not near the University's Chapel Hill campus, you may take your exam under supervision at an accredited college, university, community college, or technical institute. For more information, contact:

Independent Studies
CB #1020, The Friday Center
UNC-Chapel Hill
Chapel Hill, NC 27599-1020
1(800) 862-5669 / (919) 962-1134

The Thomas Edison College Examination Program offers more than 50 exams in liberal arts, business, and professional areas. Thomas Edison State College administers tests twice a month in Trenton, New Jersey; however, students may arrange to take their tests with a proctor at any accredited American college or university or U.S. military base. Most of the tests are multiple choice; some also include short answer or essay questions. Time limits range from 90 minutes to 4 hours, depending on the exam. For more information, contact:

Thomas Edison State College
TECEP, Office of Testing and Assessment
101 W. State Street
Trenton, NJ 08608-1176
(609) 633-2844

New York University's Foreign Language Program offers proficiency exams in more than 40 languages, from Albanian to Yiddish. Two exams are available in each language: The 12-point test is equivalent to 4 undergraduate semesters, and the 16-point exam may lead to upper level credit. The tests are given at the university's Foreign Language Department throughout the year.

Proof of foreign language proficiency does not guarantee college credit. Some colleges and universities accept transcripts only for languages commonly taught, such as French and Spanish. Nontraditional programs are more likely than traditional ones to grant credit for proficiency in other languages.

For an informational brochure and registration form for NYU's foreign language proficiency exams, contact:

New York University
Foreign Language Department
48 Cooper Square, Room 107
New York, NY 10003
(212) 998-7030

Government institutes:

The Defense Language Institute and Foreign Service Institute administer foreign language proficiency exams for personnel stationed abroad. Usually, the tests are given at the end of intensive language courses or upon completion of service overseas. But some people – like Jorge, who knows Spanish – speak another language fluently and may be allowed to take a proficiency exam in that language before completing their tour of duty. Contact one of the offices listed below to obtain transcripts of those scores. Proof of proficiency does not guarantee college credit, however, as discussed above.

To request score reports from the Defense Language Institute for Defense Language Proficiency Tests, send your name, Social Security number, language for which you were tested, and, most importantly, when and where you took the exam to:

Commandant, Defense Language Institute
Attn: ATFL-ES-T
DLPT Score Report Request
Presidio of Monterey
Monterey, CA 93944-5006

To request transcripts of scores for Foreign Service Institute exams, send your name, Social Security number, language for which you were tested, and dates or year of exams to:

Foreign Service Institute
Arlington Hall
4020 Arlington Boulevard
Rosslyn, VA 22204-1500
Attn: Testing Office (Send your request to the attention of the testing office of the foreign language in which you were tested)

Credit For Experience

Experiential learning credit may be given for knowledge gained through job responsibilities, personal hobbies, volunteer opportunities, homemaking, and other experiences. Colleges and universities base credit awards on the knowledge you have attained, not for the experience alone. In addition, the knowledge must be college level; not just any learning will do. Throwing horseshoes as a hobby is not likely to be worth college credit. But if you've done research on how and where the sport originated, visited blacksmiths, organized tournaments, and written a column for a trade journal – well, that's a horseshoe of a different color.

Adults attempting to get credit for their experience should be forewarned: Having your experience evaluated for college credit is time-consuming, tedious work – not an easy shortcut for people who want quick-fix college credits. And not all experience, no matter how valuable, is the equivalent of college courses.

Requesting college credit for your experiential learning can be tricky. You should get assistance from a credit evaluations officer at the school you plan to attend, but you should also have a general idea of what your knowledge is worth. A common method for converting knowledge into credit is to use a college catalog. Find course titles and descriptions that match what you have learned through experience, and request the number of credits offered for those courses.

Once you know what credit to ask for, you must usually present your case in writing to officials at the college you plan to attend. The most common form of presenting experiential learning for credit is the portfolio. A portfolio is a written record of your knowledge along with a request for equivalent college credit. It includes an identification and description of the knowledge for which you are requesting credit, an explanatory essay of how the knowledge was gained and how it fits into your educational plans, documentation that you have acquired such knowledge, and a request for college credit. Required elements of a portfolio vary by schools but generally follow those guidelines.

In identifying knowledge you have gained, be specific about exactly what you have learned. For example, it is not enough for Lynette to say she runs a business. She must identify the knowledge she has gained from running it, such as personnel management, tax law, marketing strategy, and inventory review. She must also include brief descriptions about her knowledge of each to support her claims of having those skills.

The essay gives you a chance to relay something about who you are. It should address your educational goals, include relevant autobiographical details, and be well organized, neat, and convey confidence. In his essay, Jorge might first state his goal of becoming an engineer. Then he would explain why he joined the Army, where he got hands-on training and experience in developing and servicing electronic equipment.

This, he would say, led to his hobby of creating remote-controlled model cars, of which he has built 20. His conclusion would highlight his accomplishments and tie them to his desire to become an electronic engineer.

Documentation is evidence that you've learned what you claim to have learned. You can show proof of knowledge in a variety of ways, including audio or video recordings, letters from current or former employers describing your specific duties and job performance, blueprints, photographs or artwork, and transcripts of certifying exams for professional licenses and certification – such as Alice's certification from the American Culinary Federation. Although documentation can take many forms, written proof alone is not always enough. If it is impossible to document your knowledge in writing, find out if your experiential learning can be assessed through supplemental oral exams by a faculty expert.

Earning a College Degree

Nontraditional students often have work, family, and financial obligations that prevent them from quitting their jobs to attend school full time. Can they still meet their educational goals? Yes.

More than 150 accredited colleges and universities have nontraditional bachelor's degree programs that require students to spend little or no time on campus; over 300 others have nontraditional campus-based degree programs. Some of those schools, as well as most junior and community colleges, offer associate's degrees nontraditionally. Each school with a nontraditional course of study determines its own rules for awarding credit for prior coursework, exams, or experience, as discussed previously. Most have charges on top of tuition for providing these special services.

Several publications profile nontraditional degree programs; see the Resources section at the end of this article for more information. To determine which school best fits your academic profile and educational goals, first list your criteria. Then, evaluate nontraditional programs based on their accreditation, features, residency requirements, and expenses. Once you have chosen several schools to explore further, write to them for more information. Detailed explanations of school policies should help you decide which ones you want to apply to.

Get beyond the printed word – especially the glowing words each school writes about itself. Check out the schools you are considering with higher education authorities, alumni, employers, family members, and friends. If possible, visit the campus to talk to students and instructors and sit in on a few classes, even if you will be completing most or all of your work off campus. Ask school officials questions about such things as enrollment numbers, graduation rate, faculty qualifications, and confusing details about the application process or academic policies. After you have thoroughly investigated each prospective college or university, you can make an informed decision about which is right for you.

Accreditation

Accreditation is a process colleges and universities submit to voluntarily for getting their credentials. An accredited school has been investigated and visited by teams of observers and has periodic inspections by a private accrediting agency. The initial review can take two years or more.

Regional agencies accredit entire schools, and professional agencies accredit either specialized schools or departments within schools. Although there are no national accrediting standards, not just any accreditation will do. Countless "accreditation associations" have been invented by schools, many of which have no academic programs and sell phony degrees, to accredit themselves. But 6 regional and about 80 professional accrediting associations in the United States are recognized by the U.S. Department of Education or the Commission on Recognition of Postsecondary Accreditation. When checking accreditation, these are the names to look for. For more information about accreditation and accrediting agencies, contact:

    Institutional Participation Oversight Service Accreditation and State Liaison Division
    U.S. Department of Education
    ROB 3, Room 3915
    600 Independence Ave., SW
    Washington, DC 20202-5244
    (202) 708-7417

Because accreditation is not mandatory, lack of accreditation does not necessarily mean a school or program is bad. Some schools choose not to apply for accreditation, are in the process of applying, or have educational methods too unconventional for an accrediting association's standards. For the nontraditional student, however, earning a degree from a college or university with recognized accreditation is an especially important consideration. Although nontraditional education is becoming more widely accepted, it is not yet mainstream. Employers skeptical of a degree earned in a nontraditional manner are likely to be even less accepting of one from an unaccredited school.

Program Features

Because nontraditional students have diverse educational objectives, nontraditional schools are diverse in what they offer. Some programs are geared toward helping students organize their scattered educational credits to get a degree as quickly as possible. Others cater to those who may have specific credits or experience but need assistance in completing requirements. Whatever your educational profile, you should look for a program that works with you in obtaining your educational goals.

A few nontraditional programs have special admissions policies for adult learners like Alice, who plan to earn their GEDs but want to enroll in college in the meantime. Other features of nontraditional programs include individualized learning agreements, intensive academic counseling, cooperative learning and internship placement, and waiver of some prerequisites or other requirements – as well as college credit for prior coursework, examinations, and experiential learning, all discussed previously.

Lynette, whose primary goal is to finish her degree, wants to earn maximum credits for her business experience. She will look for programs that do not limit the number of credits awarded for equivalency exams and experiential learning. And since well-documented proof of knowledge is essential for earning experiential learning credits, Lynette should make sure the program she chooses provides assistance to students submitting a portfolio.

Jorge, on the other hand, has more credits than he needs in certain areas and is willing to forego some. To become an engineer, he must have a bachelor's degree; but because he is accustomed to hands-on learning, Jorge is interested in getting experience as he gains more technical skills. He will concentrate on finding schools with strong cooperative education, supervised fieldwork, or internship programs.

Residency Requirements

Programs are sometimes deemed nontraditional because of their residency requirements. Many people think of residency for colleges and universities in terms of tuition, with in-state students paying less than out-of-state ones. Residency also may refer to where a student lives, either on or off campus, while attending school.

But in nontraditional education, residency usually refers to how much time students must spend on campus, regardless of whether they attend classes there. In some nontraditional programs, students need not ever step foot on campus. Others require only a very short residency, such as one day or a few weeks. Many schools have standard residency requirements of several semesters but schedule classes for evenings or weekends to accommodate working adults.

Lynette, who previously took courses by independent study, prefers to earn credits by distance study. She will focus on schools that have no residency requirement. Several colleges and universities have nonresident degree completion programs for adults with some college credit. Under the direction of a faculty advisor, students devise a plan for earning their remaining credits. Methods for earning credits include independent study, distance learning, seminars, supervised fieldwork, and group study at arranged sites. Students may have to earn a certain number of credits through the degree-granting institution. But many programs allow students to take courses at accredited schools of their choice for transfer toward their degree.

Alice wants to attend lectures but has an unpredictable schedule. Her best course of action will be to seek out short residency programs that require students to attend seminars once or twice a semester. She can take courses that are televised and videotape them to watch when her schedule permits, with the seminars helping to ensure that she properly completes her coursework. Many colleges and universities with short residency requirements also permit students to earn some credits elsewhere, by whatever means the student chooses.

Some fields of study require classroom instruction. As Jorge will discover, few colleges and universities allow students to earn a bachelor's degree in engineering entirely through independent study. Nontraditional residency programs are designed to accommodate adults' daytime work schedules. Jorge should look for programs offering evening, weekend, summer, and accelerated courses.

Tuition and Other Expenses

The final decisions about which schools Alice, Jorge, and Lynette attend may hinge in large part on a single issue: Cost. And rising tuition is only part of the equation. Beginning with application fees and continuing through graduation fees, college expenses add up.

Traditional and nontraditional students have some expenses in common, such as the cost of books and other materials. Tuition might even be the same for some courses, especially for colleges and universities offering standard ones at unusual times. But for nontraditional programs, students may also pay fees for services such as credit or transcript review, evaluation, advisement, and portfolio assessment.

Students are also responsible for postage and handling or setup expenses for independent study courses, as well as for all examination and transcript fees for transferring credits. Usually, the more nontraditional the program, the more detailed the fees. Some schools charge a yearly enrollment fee rather than tuition for degree completion candidates who want their files to remain active.

Although tuition and fees might seem expensive, most educators tell you not to let money come between you and your educational goals. Talk to someone in the financial aid department of the school you plan to attend or check your library for publications about financial aid sources. The U.S. Department of Education publishes a guide to Federal aid programs such as Pell Grants, student loans, and work-study. To order the free 74-page booklet, *The Student Guide: Financial Aid from the U.S. Department of Education,* contact:

Federal Student Aid Information Center
P.O. Box 84
Washington, DC 20044
1 (800) 4FED-AID (433-3243)

Resources

Information on how to earn a high school diploma or college degree without following the usual routes is available from several organizations and in numerous publications. Information on nontraditional graduate degree programs, available for master's through doctoral level, though not discussed in this article, can usually be obtained from the same resources that detail bachelor's degree programs.

National Learning Corporation publishes study guides for all of these exams, for both general examinations and tests in specific subject areas. To order study guides, or to browse their catalog featuring more than 5,000 titles, visit NLC online at www.passbooks.com, or contact them by phone at (800) 632-8888.

Organizations

Adult learners should always contact their local school system, community college, or university to learn about programs that are readily available. The following national organizations can also supply information:

American Council on Education
One Dupont Circle
Washington, DC 20036-1193
(202) 939-9300

Within the American Council on Education, the Center for Adult Learning and Educational Credentials administers the National External Diploma Program, the GED Program, the Program on Noncollegiate Sponsored Instruction, the Credit by Examination Program, and the Military Evaluations Program.

DANTES Subject Standardized Tests

INTRODUCTION

The DANTES (Defense Activity for Non-Traditional Education Support) subject standardized tests are comprehensive college and graduate level examinations given by the Armed Forces, colleges and graduate schools as end-of-subject course evaluation final examinations or to obtain college equivalency credits in the various subject areas tested.

The DANTES Examination Program enables students to obtain college credit for what they have learned on the job, through self-study, personal interest, correspondence courses or by any other means. It is used by colleges and universities to award college credit to students who demonstrate that they know as much as students completing an equivalent college course. It is a cost-efficient, time-saving way for students to use their knowledge to accomplish their educational goals.

Most schools accept the American Council on Education (ACE) recommendations for the minimum score required and the amount of credit awarded, but not all schools do. Be sure to check the policy regarding the score level required for credit and the number of credits to be awarded.

Not all tests are accepted by all institutions. Even when a test is accepted by an institution, it may not be acceptable for every program at that institution. Before considering testing, ascertain the acceptability of a specific test for a particular course.

Colleges and universities that administer DANTES tests may administer them to any applicant – or they may administer the tests only to students registered at their institution. Decisions about who will be allowed to test are made by the school. Students should contact the test center to determine current policies and schedules for DANTES testing.

Colleges and universities authorized to administer DANTES tests usually do so throughout the calendar year. Each school sets its own fee for test administration and establishes its own testing schedule. Contact the representative at the administering school directly to make arrangements for testing.

Checklist For Students

- ✓ Visit **www.getcollegecredit.com** to obtain a list of tests, fact sheets, test preparation materials, participating colleges and universities, and much more.

- ✓ Contact your school advisor to confirm that the DSST you selected will fit into your curriculum.

- ✓ Consult the ***DSST Candidate Information Bulletin*** for answers to specific questions.

- ✓ Contact the test site to schedule your test.

- ✓ Prepare for your examination by using the fact sheet as a guide.

- ✓ Take the test.

If you would like a score report sent to your college or university, it is a good idea to bring the four-digit code with you. You must write the DSST Test Center Code for that institution on your answer sheet at the time of testing. DSST Test Center Codes are noted in the DSST Participating Colleges and Universities listing on the Web site.

If you prefer to send a score report to an institution at a later date, there is a transcript fee of $20 for each transcript ordered.

Thomson Prometric
DSST Program
2000 Lenox Drive, Third Floor
Lawrenceville, NJ 08648

Toll-free: 877-471-9860
609-895-5011

E-mail: pnj-dsst@thomson.com

MAKING A COLLEGE DEGREE WITHIN YOUR REACH

Today, there are many educational alternatives to the classroom—you can learn from your job, your reading, your independent study, and special interests you pursue. You may already have learned the subject matter covered by some college-level courses.

The DSST Program is a nationally recognized testing program that gives you the opportunity to receive college credit for learning acquired outside the traditional college classroom. Colleges and universities throughout the United States administer the program, developed by Thomson Prometric, year-round. Annually, over 90,000 DSSTs are administered to individuals who are interested in continuing their education. Take advantage of the DSST testing program; it speeds the educational process and provides the flexibility adults need, making earning a degree more feasible.

Since requirements differ from college to college, please check with the credit-awarding institution before taking a DSST. More than 1,800 colleges and universities currently award credit for DSSTs, and the number is growing every day. You can choose from 37 test titles in the areas of Social Science, Business, Mathematics, Applied Technology, Humanities, and Physical Science. A brief description of each examination is found on the pages that follow.

Reach Your Career Goals Through DSSTs

Use DSSTs to help you earn your degree, get a promotion, or simply demonstrate that you have college-level knowledge in subjects relevant to your work.

Save Time...

You don't have to sit through classes when you have previously acquired the knowledge or experience for most of what is being taught and can learn the rest yourself. You might be able to bypass introductory-level courses in subject areas you already know.

Save Money...

DSSTs save you money because the classes you bypass by earning credit through the DSST Program are classes you won't have to pay for on your way to earning your degree. You can use the money instead to take more advanced courses that can be more challenging and rewarding.

Improve Your Chances for Admission to College

Each college has its own admission policies; however, having passing scores for DSSTs on your transcript can provide strong evidence of how well you can perform at the college level.

Gain Confidence Performing at a College Level

Many adults returning to college find that lack of confidence is often the greatest hurdle to overcome. Passing a DSST demonstrates your ability to perform on a college level.

Make Up for Courses You May Have Missed

You may be ready to graduate from college and find that you are a few credits short of earning your degree. By using semester breaks, vacation time, or leisure time to study independently, you can prepare to take one or more DSSTs, fulfill your academic requirements, and graduate on time.

If You Cannot Attend Regularly Scheduled Classes...

If your lifestyle or responsibilities prevent you from attending regularly scheduled classes, you can earn your college degree from a college offering an external degree program. The DSST Program allows you to earn your degree by study and experience outside the traditional classroom.

Many colleges and universities offer external degree or distance learning programs. For additional information, contact the college you plan to attend or:

Center for Lifelong Learning
American Council on Education
One DuPont Circle NW, Suite 250
Washington, DC 20036
202-939-9475
www.acenet.edu
(Select "Center for Lifelong Learning" under "Programs & Services"
for more information)

Fact Sheets

For each test, there is a Fact Sheet that outlines the topics covered by each test and includes a list of sample questions, a list of recommended references of books that would be useful for review, and the number of credits awarded for a passing score as recommended by the American Council on Education (ACE). *Please note that some schools require scores that are higher than the minimum ACE-recommended passing score.* It is suggested that you check with your college or university to determine what score they require in order to earn credit. You can obtain Fact Sheets by:

- Downloading them from www.getcollegecredit.com
- E-mailing a request to pnj-dsst@thomson.com
- Completing a Candidate Publications Order Form

DSST Online Practice Tests

DSST online practice tests contain items that reflect a *partial range of difficulty* identified in the Content Outline section on each Fact Sheet. There is an online DSST Practice Test in the following categories:

- Mathematics
- Social Science
- Business
- Physical Science
- Applied Technology
- Humanities

Although the online DSST Practice Test questions do not indicate the full range of difficulty you would find in an actual DSST test, they will help you assess your knowledge level. Each online DSST Practice Test can be purchased by visiting www.getcollegecredit.com and clicking on DSST Practice Exams.

TAKING DSST EXAMINATIONS

Earning College Credit for DSST Examinations

To find out if the college of your choice awards credit for passing DSST scores, contact the admissions office or counseling and testing office. The college can also provide information on the scores required for awarding credit, the number of credit hours awarded, and any courses that can be bypassed with satisfactory scores.

It is important that you contact the institution of your choice as early as possible since credit-awarding policies differ among colleges and universities.

Where to Take DSSTs

DSSTs are administered at colleges and universities nationwide. Each location determines the frequency and scheduling of test administrations. To obtain the most current list of participating DSST colleges and universities:
- Visit and download the information from www.getcollegecredit.com
- E-mail pnj-dsst@thomson.com

Scheduling Your Examination

Please be aware that some colleges and universities provide DSST testing services to enrolled students only. After you have selected a college or university that administers DSSTs, you will need to contact them to schedule your test date.

The fee to take a DSST is $60 per test. This fee entitles you to two score reports after the test is scored. One will be sent directly to you and the other will be sent to the college or university that you designate on your answer sheet. You may pay the test fee with a certified check or U.S. money order made payable to Thomson Prometric or you may charge the test fee to your Visa, MasterCard or American Express credit card. Note: The credit card statement will reflect a charge from Thomson Prometric for all DSST examinations. *(Declined credit card charges will be assessed an additional $25 processing fee.)*

In addition, the test site may also require a test administration fee for each examination, to be paid directly to the institution. Contact the test site to determine its administration fee and payment policy.

Other Testing Arrangements

If you are unable to find a participating DSST college or university in your area, you may want to contact the testing office of a local accredited college or university to determine whether a representative from that office will agree to administer the test(s) for you.

The school's representative should then contact the DSST Program at 866-794-3497 to arrange for this administration. If you are unable to locate a test site, contact Thomson Prometric for assistance at pnj-dsst@thomson.com or 866-794-3497.

Testing Accommodations for Students with Disabilities

Thomson Prometric is committed to serving test takers with disabilities by providing services and reasonable testing accommodations as set forth in the provisions of the *Americans with Disabilities Act* (ADA). If you have a disability, as prescribed by the ADA, and require special testing services or arrangements, please contact the test administrator at the test site. You will be asked to submit to the test administrator documentation of your disability and your request for special accommodations. The test administrator will then forward your documentation along with your request for testing accommodations to Thomson Prometric for approval.

Please submit your request as far in advance of your test date as possible so that the necessary accommodations can be made. Only test takers with documented disabilities are eligible for special accommodations.

On the Day of the Examination

It is important to review this information and to have the correct identification present on the day of the examination:

- Arrive on time as a courtesy to the test administrator.
- Bring a valid form of government-issued identification that includes a current photo and your signature (acceptable documents include a driver's license, passport, state-issued identification card or military identification). *Anyone who fails to present valid identification will not be allowed to test.*
- Bring several No. 2 (soft-lead) sharpened pencils with good erasers, a watch, and a black pen if you will be writing an essay.
- Do not bring books or papers.
- Do not bring an alarm watch that beeps, a telephone, or a phone beeper into the testing room.
- The use of nonprogrammable calculators, slide rules, scratch paper and/or other materials is permitted for some of the tests.

DSST SCORING POLICIES

Your DSST examination scores are reported only to you, unless you request that they be sent elsewhere. If you want your scores sent to your college, you must provide the correct DSST code number of the school on your answer sheet at the time you take the test. See the *DSST Directory of Colleges and Universities* on the Web site www.getcollegecredit.com.

If your institution is not listed, contact Thomson Prometric at 866-794-3497 to establish a code number. (Some schools may require a student to be enrolled prior to receiving a score report.)

Receiving Your Score Report

Allow approximately four weeks after testing to receive your score report.

Calling DSST Customer Service before the required four-week score processing time has elapsed will not expedite the processing of your scores. Due to privacy and security requirements, scores will not be reported to students over the telephone under any circumstance.

Scoring of Principles of Public Speaking Speeches

The speech portion of the *Principles of Public Speaking* examination will be sent to speech raters who are faculty members at accredited colleges that currently teach or have previously taught the course. Scores for the *Principles of Public Speaking* examination are available six to eight weeks from receipt by Thomson Prometric. If you take the *Principles of Public Speaking* examination and fail (either the objective, speech portion, or both), you must follow the retesting policy waiting period of six months (180 days) before retaking the entire exam.

Essays

The essays for *Ethics in America* and *Technical Writing* are optional and thus are not scored by raters. The essays are forwarded to the college or university that you designate, along with your score report, for their use in determining the award of credit. Before taking the *Ethics in America* or *Technical Writing* examinations, check with your college or university to determine whether the essay is required.

NOTE: *Principles of Public Speaking* speech topic cassette tapes and essays are kept on file at Thomson Prometric for one year from the date of administration.

How to Get Transcripts

There is a $20 fee for each transcript you request. Payment must be in the form of a certified check, U.S. money order payable to Thomson Prometric, or credit card. Personal checks and debit cards are NOT an acceptable method of payment. One transcript may include scores for one or more examinations taken. To request a transcript, download the Transcript Order Form from www.getcollegecredit.com.

DESCRIPTION OF THE DSST EXAMINATIONS

Mathematics

• **Fundamentals of College Algebra** covers mathematical concepts such as fundamental algebraic operations; linear, absolute value; quadratic equations, inequalities, radials, exponents and logarithms, factoring polynomials and graphing. The use of a nonprogrammable, handheld calculator is permitted.

• **Principles of Statistics** tests the understanding of the various topics of statistics, both qualitatively and quantitatively, and the ability to apply statistical methods to solve a variety of problems. The topics included in this test are descriptive statistics; correlation and regression; probability; chance models and sampling and tests of significance. The use of a nonprogrammable, handheld calculator is permitted.

Social Science

• **Art of the Western World** deals with the history of art during the following periods: classical; Romanesque and Gothic; early Renaissance; high Renaissance, Baroque; rococo; neoclassicism and romanticism; realism, impressionism and post-impressionism; early twentieth century; and post-World War II.

• **Western Europe Since 1945** tests the knowledge of basic facts and terms and the understanding of concepts and principles related to the areas of the historical background of the aftermath of the Second World War and rebuilding of Europe; national political systems; issues and policies in Western European societies; European institutions and processes; and Europe's relations with the rest of the world.

• **An Introduction to the Modern Middle East** emphasizes core knowledge (including geography, Judaism, Christianity, Islam, ethnicity); nineteenth-century European impact; twentieth-century Western influences; World Wars I and II; new nations; social and cultural changes (1900-1960) and the Middle East from 1960 to present.

• **Human/Cultural Geography** includes the Earth and basic facts (coordinate systems, maps, physiography, atmosphere, soils and vegetation, water); culture and environment, spatial processes (social processes, modern economic systems, settlement patterns, political geography); and regional geography.

- **Rise and Fall of the Soviet Union** covers Russia under the Old Regime; the Revolutionary Period; New Economic Policy; Pre-war Stalinism; The Second World War; Post-war Stalinism; The Khrushchev Years; The Brezhnev Era; and reform and collapse.

- **A History of the Vietnam War** covers the history of the roots of the Vietnam War; the First Vietnam War (1946-1954); pre-war developments (1954-1963); American involvement in the Vietnam War; Tet (1968); Vietnamizing the War (1968-1973); Cambodia and Laos; peace; legacies and lessons.

- **The Civil War and Reconstruction** covers the Civil War from presecession (1861) through Reconstruction. It includes causes of the war; secession; Fort Sumter; the war in the east and in the west; major battles; the political situation; assassination of Lincoln; end of the Confederacy; and Reconstruction.

- **Foundations of Education** includes topics such as contemporary issues in education; past and current influences on education (philosophies, democratic ideals, social/economic influences); and the interrelationships between contemporary issues and influences.

- **Life-span Developmental Psychology** covers models and theories; methods of study; ethical issues; biological development; perception, learning and memory; cognition and language; social, emotional, and personality development; social behaviors, family life cycle, extrafamilial settings; singlehood and cohabitation; occupational development and retirement; adjustment to life stresses; and bereavement and loss.

- **Drug and Alcohol Abuse** includes such topics as drug use in society; classification of drugs; pharmacological principles; alcohol (types, effects of, alcoholism); general principles and use of sedative hypnotics, narcotic analgesics, stimulants, and hallucinogens; other drugs (inhalants, steroids); and prevention/treatment.

- **General Anthropology** deals with anthropology as a discipline; theoretical perspectives; physical anthropology; archaeology; social organization; economic organization; political organization; religion; and modernization and application of anthropology.

- **Introduction to Law Enforcement** includes topics such as history and professional movement of law enforcement; overview of the U.S. criminal justice system; police systems in the U.S.; police organization, management, and issues; and U.S. law and precedents.

- **Criminal Justice** deals with criminal behavior (crime in the U.S., theories of crime, types of crime); the criminal justice system (historical origins, legal foundations, due process); police; the court system (history and organization, adult court system, juvenile court, pre-trial and post-trial processes); and corrections.

- **Fundamentals of Counseling** covers historical development (significant influences and people); counselor roles and functions; the counseling relationship; and theoretical approaches to counseling.

Business
- **Principles of Finance** deals with financial statements and planning; time value of money; working capital management; valuation and characteristics; capital budgeting; cost of capital; risk and return; and international financial management. The use of a nonprogrammable, handheld calculator is permitted.

- **Principles of Financial Accounting** includes topics such as general concepts and principles, accounting cycle and classification; transaction analysis; accruals and deferrals; cash and internal control; current accounts; long- and short-term liabilities; capital stock; and financial statements. The use of a nonprogrammable, handheld calculator is permitted.

- **Human Resource Management** covers general employment issues; job analysis; training and development; performance appraisals; compensation issues; security issues; personnel legislation and regulation; labor relations and current issues; an overview of the Human Resource Management Field; Human Resource Planning; Staffing; training and development; compensation issues; safety and health; employee rights and discipline; employment law; labor relations and current issues and trends.

- **Organizational Behavior** deals with the study of organizational behavior (scientific approaches, research designs, data collection methods); individual processes and characteristics; interpersonal and group processes and characteristics; organizational processes and characteristics; and change and development processes.

- **Principles of Supervision** deals with the roles and responsibilities of the supervisor; management functions (planning, organization and staffing, directing at the supervisory level); and other topics (legal issues, stress management, union environments, quality concerns).

- **Business Law II** covers topics such as sales of goods; debtor and creditor relations; business organizations; property; and commercial paper.

- **Introduction to Computing** includes topics such as history and technological generations; hardware/software; applications to information technology; program development; data management; communications and connectivity; and computing and society. The use of a nonprogrammable, handheld calculator is permitted.

- **Management Information Systems** covers systems theory, analysis and design of systems, hardware and software; database management; telecommunications; management of the MIS functional area and informational support.

- **Introduction to Business** deals with economic issues affecting business; international business; government and business; forms of business ownership; small business, entrepreneurship and franchise; management process; human resource management; production and operations; marketing management; financial management; risk management and insurance; and management and information systems.

- **Money and Banking** covers the role and kinds of money; commercial banks and other financial intermediaries; central banking and the Federal Reserve system; money and macroeconomics activity; monetary policy in the U.S.; and the international monetary system.

- **Personal Finance** includes topics such as financial goals and values; budgeting; credit and debt; major purchases; taxes; insurance; investments; and retirement and estate planning. The use of auxiliary materials, such as calculators and slide rules, is NOT permitted.

- **Business Mathematics** deals with basic operations with integers, fractions, and decimals; round numbers; ratios; averages; business graphs; simple interest; compound interest and annuities; net pay and deductions; discounts and markups; depreciation and net worth; corporate securities; distribution of ownership; and stock and asset turnover.

Physical Science

- **Astronomy** covers the history of astronomy, celestial mechanics; celestial systems; astronomical instruments; the solar system; nature and evolution; the galaxy; the universe; determining astronomical distances; and life in the universe.

- **Here's to Your Health** covers mental health and behavior; human development and relationships; substance abuse; fitness and nutrition; risk factors, disease, and disease prevention; and safety, consumer awareness, and environmental concerns.

- **Environment and Humanity** deals with topics such as ecological concepts (ecosystems, global ecology, food chains and webs); environmental impacts; environmental management and conservation; and political processes and the future.

- **Principles of Physical Science I** includes physics: Newton's Laws of Motion; energy and momentum; thermodynamics; wave and optics; electricity and magnetism; chemistry: properties of matter; atomic theory and structure; and chemical reactions.

- **Physical Geology** covers Earth materials; igneous, sedimentary, and metamorphic rocks; surface processes (weathering, groundwater, glaciers, oceanic systems, deserts and winds, hydrologic cycle); internal Earth processes; and applications (mineral and energy resources, environmental geology).

Applied Technology

- **Technical Writing** covers topics such as theory and practice of technical writing; purpose, content, and organizational patterns of common types of technical documents; elements of various technical reports; and technical editing. Students have the option to write a short essay on one of the technical topics provided. Thomson Prometric will not score the essay; however, for determining the award of credit, a copy of the essay will be forwarded to the college or university you've designated along with the score report or transcript.

Humanities

- **Ethics in America** deals with ethical traditions (Greek views, Biblical traditions, moral law, consequential ethics, feminist ethics); ethical analysis of issues arising in interpersonal and personal-societal relationships and in professional and occupational roles; and relationships between ethical traditions and the ethical analysis of situations. Students have the option to write an essay to analyze a morally problematic situation in terms of issues relevant to a decision and arguments for alternative positions. Thomson Prometric will not score the essay; however, for determining the award of credit, a copy of the essay will be forwarded to the college or university you've designated along with the score report or transcript.

- **Introduction to World Religions** covers topics such as dimensions and approaches to religion; primal religions; Hinduism; Buddhism; Confucianism; Taoism; Judaism; Christianity; and Islam.

- **Principles of Public Speaking** consists of two parts: Part One consists of multiple-choice questions covering considerations of Principles of Public Speaking; audience analysis; purposes of speeches; structure/organization; content/supporting materials; research; language and style; delivery; communication apprehension; listening and feedback; and criticism and evaluation. Part Two requires the student to record an impromptu persuasive speech that will be scored.

FREQUENTLY ASKED QUESTIONS ABOUT DSSTs

In order to pass the test, must I study from one of the recommended references?

The recommended references are a listing of books that were being used as textbooks in college courses of the same or similar title at the time the test was developed. Appropriate textbooks for study are not limited to those listed in the fact sheet. If you wish to obtain study resources to prepare for the examination, you may reference either the current edition of the listed titles or textbooks currently used at a local college or university for the same class title. It is recommended that you reference more than one textbook on the topics outlined in the fact sheet. You should begin by checking textbook content against the content outline included on the front page of the DSST fact sheet before selecting textbooks that cover the text content from which to study. Textbooks may be found at the campus bookstore of a local college or university offering a course on the subject.

Is there a penalty for guessing on the tests?

There is no penalty for guessing on DSSTs, so you should mark an answer for each question.

How much time will I have to complete the test?

Many DSSTs can be completed within 90 minutes; however, additional time can be allowed if necessary.

What should I do if I find a test question irregularity?

Continue testing and then report the irregularity to the test administrator after the test. This may be done by asking that the test administrator note the irregularity on the Supervisor's Irregularity Report or you can write to Thomson Prometric, DSST Program, 2000 Lenox Drive, Third Floor, Lawrenceville, NJ 08648, and indicate the form and question number(s) or circumstances as well as your name and address.

When will I receive my score report?

Allow approximately four weeks from the date of testing to receive your score report. Allow six to eight weeks to receive a score report for the *Principles of Public Speaking* examination.

Will my test scores be released without my permission?

Your test score will not be released to anyone other than the school you designate on your answer sheet unless you write to us and ask us to send a transcript elsewhere. Instructions about how to do this can be found on your score report. Your scores may be used for research purposes, but individual scores are never made public nor are individuals identified if research findings are made public.

If I do not achieve a passing score on the test, how long must I wait until I can take the test again?

If you do not receive a score on the test that will enable you to obtain credit for the course, you may take the test again after six months (180 days). Please do not attempt to take the test before six months (180 days) have passed because you will receive a score report marked *invalid* and your test fee will not be refunded.

Can my test scores be canceled?

The test administrator is required to report any irregularities to Thomson Prometric. <u>The consequence of bringing unauthorized materials into the testing room, or giving or receiving help, will be the forfeiture of your test fee and the invalidation of test scores.</u> The DSST Program reserves the right to cancel scores and not issue score reports in such situations.

What can I do if I feel that my test scores were not accurately reported?

Thomson Prometric recognizes the extreme importance of test results to candidates and has a multi-step quality-control procedure to help ensure that reported scores are accurate. If you have reason to believe that your score(s) were not accurately reported, you may request to have your answer sheet reviewed and hand scored.

The fees for this service are:
- $20 fee if requested within six months of the test date
- $30 fee if requested more than six months from the test date
- $30 fee if a re-evaluation of the *Principles of Public Speaking* speech is requested

The fee for this service can be paid by credit card or by certified check or U.S. money order payable to Thomson Prometric. Submit your request for score verification along with the appropriate fee or credit card information (credit card number and expiration date) to Thomson Prometric, DSST Program, 2000 Lenox Drive, Third Floor, Lawrenceville, NJ 08648. Include your full name, the test title, the date you took the test, and your Social Security number. Candidates will be notified if a scoring discrepancy is discovered within four weeks of receipt of the request.

What does ACE recommendation mean?

The ACE recommendation is the minimum passing score recommended by the American Council on Education for any given test. It is equivalent to the average score of students in the DSST norming sample who received a grade of C for the course. Some schools require a score higher than the ACE recommendation.

Who is NLC?

National Learning Corporation (NLC) has been successfully preparing candidates for 40 years for over 5,000 exams. NLC publishes Passbook® study guides to help candidates prepare for all DANTES and CLEP exams and almost every other type of exam from high school through adult career.

Go to our website — www.passbooks.com — or call (800) 632-8888 for information about ordering our Passbooks.

To get detailed information on the DSST program and DSST preparation materials, visit www.getcollegecredit.com.

If you are interested in taking the DSST exams, call 877-471-9860 or e-mail pnj-dsst@thomson.com.

HOW TO TAKE A TEST

You have studied long, hard and conscientiously.

With your official admission card in hand, and your heart pounding, you have been admitted to the examination room.

You note that there are several hundred other applicants in the examination room waiting to take the same test.

They all appear to be equally well prepared.

You know that nothing but your best effort will suffice. The "moment of truth" is at hand: you now have to demonstrate objectively, in writing, your knowledge of content and your understanding of subject matter.

You are fighting the most important battle of your life—to pass and/or score high on an examination which will determine your career and provide the economic basis for your livelihood.

What extra, special things should you know and should you do in taking the examination?

I. YOU MUST PASS AN EXAMINATION

A. WHAT EVERY CANDIDATE SHOULD KNOW
   Examination applicants often ask us for help in preparing for the written test. What can I study in advance? What kinds of questions will be asked? How will the test be given? How will the papers be graded?

B. HOW ARE EXAMS DEVELOPED?
   Examinations are carefully written by trained technicians who are specialists in the field known as "psychological measurement," in consultation with recognized authorities in the field of work that the test will cover. These experts recommend the subject matter areas or skills to be tested; only those knowledges or skills important to your success on the job are included. The most reliable books and source materials available are used as references. Together, the experts and technicians judge the difficulty level of the questions.
   Test technicians know how to phrase questions so that the problem is clearly stated. Their ethics do not permit "trick" or "catch" questions. Questions may have been tried out on sample groups, or subjected to statistical analysis, to determine their usefulness.
   Written tests are often used in combination with performance tests, ratings of training and experience, and oral interviews. All of these measures combine to form the best-known means of finding the right person for the right job.

II. HOW TO PASS THE WRITTEN TEST

A. BASIC STEPS

1) Study the announcement

How, then, can you know what subjects to study? Our best answer is: "Learn as much as possible about the class of positions for which you've applied." The exam will test the knowledge, skills and abilities needed to do the work.

Your most valuable source of information about the position you want is the official exam announcement. This announcement lists the training and experience qualifications. Check these standards and apply only if you come reasonably close to meeting them. Many jurisdictions preview the written test in the exam announcement by including a section called "Knowledge and Abilities Required," "Scope of the Examination," or some similar heading. Here you will find out specifically what fields will be tested.

2) Choose appropriate study materials

If the position for which you are applying is technical or advanced, you will read more advanced, specialized material. If you are already familiar with the basic principles of your field, elementary textbooks would waste your time. Concentrate on advanced textbooks and technical periodicals. Think through the concepts and review difficult problems in your field.

These are all general sources. You can get more ideas on your own initiative, following these leads. For example, training manuals and publications of the government agency which employs workers in your field can be useful, particularly for technical and professional positions. A letter or visit to the government department involved may result in more specific study suggestions, and certainly will provide you with a more definite idea of the exact nature of the position you are seeking.

3) Study this book!

III. KINDS OF TESTS

Tests are used for purposes other than measuring knowledge and ability to perform specified duties. For some positions, it is equally important to test ability to make adjustments to new situations or to profit from training. In others, basic mental abilities not dependent on information are essential. Questions which test these things may not appear as pertinent to the duties of the position as those which test for knowledge and information. Yet they are often highly important parts of a fair examination. For very general questions, it is almost impossible to help you direct your study efforts. What we can do is to point out some of the more common of these general abilities needed in public service positions and describe some typical questions.

1) General information

Broad, general information has been found useful for predicting job success in some kinds of work. This is tested in a variety of ways, from vocabulary lists to questions about current events. Basic background in some field of work, such as sociology or economics, may be sampled in a group of questions. Often these are principles which have become familiar to most persons through exposure rather than through formal training. It is difficult to advise you how to study for these questions; being alert to the world around you is our best suggestion.

2) Verbal ability

An example of an ability needed in many positions is verbal or language ability. Verbal ability is, in brief, the ability to use and understand words. Vocabulary and grammar tests are typical measures of this ability. Reading comprehension or paragraph interpretation questions are common in many kinds of civil service tests. You are given a paragraph of written material and asked to find its central meaning.

IV. KINDS OF QUESTIONS

1. Multiple-choice Questions

Most popular of the short-answer questions is the "multiple choice" or "best answer" question. It can be used, for example, to test for factual knowledge, ability to solve problems or judgment in meeting situations found at work.

A multiple-choice question is normally one of three types:
- It can begin with an incomplete statement followed by several possible endings. You are to find the one ending which best completes the statement, although some of the others may not be entirely wrong.
- It can also be a complete statement in the form of a question which is answered by choosing one of the statements listed.
- It can be in the form of a problem – again you select the best answer.

Here is an example of a multiple-choice question with a discussion which should give you some clues as to the method for choosing the right answer:

When an employee has a complaint about his assignment, the action which will best help him overcome his difficulty is to
- A. discuss his difficulty with his coworkers
- B. take the problem to the head of the organization
- C. take the problem to the person who gave him the assignment
- D. say nothing to anyone about his complaint

In answering this question, you should study each of the choices to find which is best. Consider choice "A" – Certainly an employee may discuss his complaint with fellow employees, but no change or improvement can result, and the complaint remains unresolved. Choice "B" is a poor choice since the head of the organization probably does not know what assignment you have been given, and taking your problem to him is known as "going over the head" of the supervisor. The supervisor, or person who made the assignment, is the person who can clarify it or correct any injustice. Choice "C" is, therefore, correct. To say nothing, as in choice "D," is unwise. Supervisors have and interest in knowing the problems employees are facing, and the employee is seeking a solution to his problem.

2. True/False

3. Matching Questions

Matching an answer from a column of choices within another column.

V. RECORDING YOUR ANSWERS

Computer terminals are used more and more today for many different kinds of exams.

For an examination with very few applicants, you may be told to record your answers in the test booklet itself. Separate answer sheets are much more common. If this separate answer sheet is to be scored by machine – and this is often the case – it is highly important that you mark your answers correctly in order to get credit.

VI. BEFORE THE TEST

YOUR PHYSICAL CONDITION IS IMPORTANT

If you are not well, you can't do your best work on tests. If you are half asleep, you can't do your best either. Here are some tips:

1) Get about the same amount of sleep you usually get. Don't stay up all night before the test, either partying or worrying—DON'T DO IT!
2) If you wear glasses, be sure to wear them when you go to take the test. This goes for hearing aids, too.
3) If you have any physical problems that may keep you from doing your best, be sure to tell the person giving the test. If you are sick or in poor health, you relay cannot do your best on any test. You can always come back and take the test some other time.

Common sense will help you find procedures to follow to get ready for an examination. Too many of us, however, overlook these sensible measures. Indeed, nervousness and fatigue have been found to be the most serious reasons why applicants fail to do their best on civil service tests. Here is a list of reminders:

- Begin your preparation early – Don't wait until the last minute to go scurrying around for books and materials or to find out what the position is all about.
- Prepare continuously – An hour a night for a week is better than an all-night cram session. This has been definitely established. What is more, a night a week for a month will return better dividends than crowding your study into a shorter period of time.
- Locate the place of the exam – You have been sent a notice telling you when and where to report for the examination. If the location is in a different town or otherwise unfamiliar to you, it would be well to inquire the best route and learn something about the building.
- Relax the night before the test – Allow your mind to rest. Do not study at all that night. Plan some mild recreation or diversion; then go to bed early and get a good night's sleep.
- Get up early enough to make a leisurely trip to the place for the test – This way unforeseen events, traffic snarls, unfamiliar buildings, etc. will not upset you.
- Dress comfortably – A written test is not a fashion show. You will be known by number and not by name, so wear something comfortable.
- Leave excess paraphernalia at home – Shopping bags and odd bundles will get in your way. You need bring only the items mentioned in the official notice you received; usually everything you need is provided. Do not bring reference books to the exam. They will only confuse those last minutes and be taken away from you when in the test room.

- Arrive somewhat ahead of time – If because of transportation schedules you must get there very early, bring a newspaper or magazine to take your mind off yourself while waiting.
- Locate the examination room – When you have found the proper room, you will be directed to the seat or part of the room where you will sit. Sometimes you are given a sheet of instructions to read while you are waiting. Do not fill out any forms until you are told to do so; just read them and be prepared.
- Relax and prepare to listen to the instructions
- If you have any physical problem that may keep you from doing your best, be sure to tell the test administrator. If you are sick or in poor health, you really cannot do your best on the exam. You can come back and take the test some other time.

VII. AT THE TEST

The day of the test is here and you have the test booklet in your hand. The temptation to get going is very strong. Caution! There is more to success than knowing the right answers. You must know how to identify your papers and understand variations in the type of short-answer question used in this particular examination. Follow these suggestions for maximum results from your efforts:

1) Cooperate with the monitor

The test administrator has a duty to create a situation in which you can be as much at ease as possible. He will give instructions, tell you when to begin, check to see that you are marking your answer sheet correctly, and so on. He is not there to guard you, although he will see that your competitors do not take unfair advantage. He wants to help you do your best.

2) Listen to all instructions

Don't jump the gun! Wait until you understand all directions. In most civil service tests you get more time than you need to answer the questions. So don't be in a hurry. Read each word of instructions until you clearly understand the meaning. Study the examples, listen to all announcements and follow directions. Ask questions if you do not understand what to do.

3) Identify your papers

Civil service exams are usually identified by number only. You will be assigned a number; you must not put your name on your test papers. Be sure to copy your number correctly. Since more than one exam may be given, copy your exact examination title.

4) Plan your time

Unless you are told that a test is a "speed" or "rate of work" test, speed itself is usually not important. Time enough to answer all the questions will be provided, but this does not mean that you have all day. An overall time limit has been set. Divide the total time (in minutes) by the number of questions to determine the approximate time you have for each question.

5) Do not linger over difficult questions

If you come across a difficult question, mark it with a paper clip (useful to have along) and come back to it when you have been through the booklet. One caution if you do this – be sure to skip a number on your answer sheet as well. Check often to be sure that you have not lost your place and that you are marking in the row numbered the same as the question you are answering.

6) Read the questions

Be sure you know what the question asks! Many capable people are unsuccessful because they failed to read the questions correctly.

7) Answer all questions

Unless you have been instructed that a penalty will be deducted for incorrect answers, it is better to guess than to omit a question.

8) Speed tests

It is often better NOT to guess on speed tests. It has been found that on timed tests people are tempted to spend the last few seconds before time is called in marking answers at random – without even reading them – in the hope of picking up a few extra points. To discourage this practice, the instructions may warn you that your score will be "corrected" for guessing. That is, a penalty will be applied. The incorrect answers will be deducted from the correct ones, or some other penalty formula will be used.

9) Review your answers

If you finish before time is called, go back to the questions you guessed or omitted to give them further thought. Review other answers if you have time.

10) Return your test materials

If you are ready to leave before others have finished or time is called, take ALL your materials to the monitor and leave quietly. Never take any test material with you. The monitor can discover whose papers are not complete, and taking a test booklet may be grounds for disqualification.

VIII. EXAMINATION TECHNIQUES

1) Read the general instructions carefully. These are usually printed on the first page of the exam booklet. As a rule, these instructions refer to the timing of the examination; the fact that you should not start work until the signal and must stop work at a signal, etc. If there are any special instructions, such as a choice of questions to be answered, make sure that you note this instruction carefully.

2) When you are ready to start work on the examination, that is as soon as the signal has been given, read the instructions to each question booklet, underline any key words or phrases, such as least, best, outline, describe and the like. In this way you will tend to answer as requested rather than discover on reviewing your paper that you listed without describing, that you selected the worst choice rather than the best choice, etc.

3) If the examination is of the objective or multiple-choice type – that is, each question will also give a series of possible answers: A, B, C or D, and you are called upon to select the best answer and write the letter next to that answer on your answer paper – it is advisable to start answering each question in turn. There may be anywhere from 50 to 100 such questions in the three or four hours allotted and you can see how much time would be taken if you read through all the questions before beginning to answer any. Furthermore, if you

come across a question or group of questions which you know would be difficult to answer, it would undoubtedly affect your handling of all the other questions.

4) If the examination is of the essay type and contains but a few questions, it is a moot point as to whether you should read all the questions before starting to answer any one. Of course, if you are given a choice – say five out of seven and the like – then it is essential to read all the questions so you can eliminate the two that are most difficult. If, however, you are asked to answer all the questions, there may be danger in trying to answer the easiest one first because you may find that you will spend too much time on it. The best technique is to answer the first question, then proceed to the second, etc.

5) Time your answers. Before the exam begins, write down the time it started, then add the time allowed for the examination and write down the time it must be completed, then divide the time available somewhat as follows:
    - If 3-1/2 hours are allowed, that would be 210 minutes. If you have 80 objective-type questions, that would be an average of 2-1/2 minutes per question. Allow yourself no more than 2 minutes per question, or a total of 160 minutes, which will permit about 50 minutes to review.
    - If for the time allotment of 210 minutes there are 7 essay questions to answer, that would average about 30 minutes a question. Give yourself only 25 minutes per question so that you have about 35 minutes to review.

6) The most important instruction is to read each question and make sure you know what is wanted. The second most important instruction is to time yourself properly so that you answer every question. The third most important instruction is to answer every question. Guess if you have to but include something for each question. Remember that you will receive no credit for a blank and will probably receive some credit if you write something in answer to an essay question. If you guess a letter – say "B" for a multiple-choice question – you may have guessed right. If you leave a blank as an answer to a multiple-choice question, the examiners may respect your feelings but it will not add a point to your score. Some exams may penalize you for wrong answers, so in such cases only, you may not want to guess unless you have some basis for your answer.

7) Suggestions
    a. Objective-type questions
        1. Examine the question booklet for proper sequence of pages and questions
        2. Read all instructions carefully
        3. Skip any question which seems too difficult; return to it after all other questions have been answered
        4. Apportion your time properly; do not spend too much time on any single question or group of questions
        5. Note and underline key words – all, most, fewest, least, best, worst, same, opposite, etc.
        6. Pay particular attention to negatives
        7. Note unusual option, e.g., unduly long, short, complex, different or similar in content to the body of the question
        8. Observe the use of "hedging" words – probably, may, most likely, etc.

9. Make sure that your answer is put next to the same number as the question
10. Do not second-guess unless you have good reason to believe the second answer is definitely more correct
11. Cross out original answer if you decide another answer is more accurate; do not erase until you are ready to hand your paper in
12. Answer all questions; guess unless instructed otherwise
13. Leave time for review

b. Essay questions
   1. Read each question carefully
   2. Determine exactly what is wanted. Underline key words or phrases.
   3. Decide on outline or paragraph answer
   4. Include many different points and elements unless asked to develop any one or two points or elements
   5. Show impartiality by giving pros and cons unless directed to select one side only
   6. Make and write down any assumptions you find necessary to answer the questions
   7. Watch your English, grammar, punctuation and choice of words
   8. Time your answers; don't crowd material

8) Answering the essay question

Most essay questions can be answered by framing the specific response around several key words or ideas. Here are a few such key words or ideas:

M's: manpower, materials, methods, money, management
P's: purpose, program, policy, plan, procedure, practice, problems, pitfalls, personnel, public relations

a. Six basic steps in handling problems:
   1. Preliminary plan and background development
   2. Collect information, data and facts
   3. Analyze and interpret information, data and facts
   4. Analyze and develop solutions as well as make recommendations
   5. Prepare report and sell recommendations
   6. Install recommendations and follow up effectiveness

b. Pitfalls to avoid
1. Taking things for granted – A statement of the situation does not necessarily imply that each of the elements is necessarily true; for example, a complaint may be invalid and biased so that all that can be taken for granted is that a complaint has been registered
2. Considering only one side of a situation – Wherever possible, indicate several alternatives and then point out the reasons you selected the best one
3. Failing to indicate follow up – Whenever your answer indicates action on your part, make certain that you will take proper follow-up action to see how successful your recommendations, procedures or actions turn out to be
4. Taking too long in answering any single question – Remember to time your answers properly

EXAMINATION SECTION

EXAMINATION SECTION
TEST 1

DIRECTIONS: Each question or incomplete statement is followed by several suggested answers or completions. Select the one that BEST answers the question or completes the statement. *PRINT THE LETTER OF THE CORRECT ANSWER IN THE SPACE AT THE RIGHT.*

1. Those who sought to transform the profession of policing primarily sought in the police reforms that took place in the United States after 1920 and lasted until 1965

    A. increased levels of public funding
    B. more extensive training programs
    C. freedom from outside influence in departmental affairs
    D. greater discretion in dealing with criminal activity

2. Which of the following court cases dealt with the issue of freedom of speech and assembly?

    A. Schenk v. United States (1919)
    B. Wolf v. Colorado (1949)
    C. Chimel v. California (1969)
    D. Brewer v. Williams (1977)

3. Approximately what percentage of United States law enforcement agencies are municipal police departments?

    A. 40   B. 60   C. 75   D. 90

4. Which of the following terms is used to denote a buyer and seller of stolen merchandise?

    A. Pawn   B. Bot   C. Fence   D. Chop shop

5. An exception to the law enforcement officer's search warrant requirement is the *plain view doctrine*. A plain view seizure must be based upon each of the following elements EXCEPT

    A. the item to be seized must be immediately apparent as contraband or evidence of a crime
    B. the officer has a valid reason to be present within the premises where the evidence is observed
    C. unexpectedly discovered evidence may be seized if the officer enters a building to search on probable cause for a crime other than the one indicated by the discovered evidence
    D. the discovery must be *inadvertent*

6. In the United States, the federal government's first involvement in actual policing was concerned with investigations involving

    A. firearms
    B. counterfeiting
    C. alcohol smuggling or *bootlegging*
    D. prostitution

1

7. Research on the occupational subculture of police reveals each of the following to be an assumption part of this subculture EXCEPT

   A. crime and criminals are most accurately identified by citizens
   B. stronger punishment will deter criminals from repeating their errors
   C. experience is better than rules
   D. the legal system is erratic; policemen make the best decisions about guilt or innocence

8. Which of the following terms is used when a prosecutor decides to drop a case after a complaint has been formally made?

   A. Nolle prosequi   B. Ex post facto
   C. Ad damnum   D. Voir dire

9. Which of the following are typical functions of most specialized police forces?
   I. Order maintenance
   II. Public services
   III. Crime prevention
   IV. Law enforcement

   The CORRECT answer is:

   A. I, II   B. II, IV   C. III, IV   D. I, III, IV

10. A conspiracy to commit fraud or other illegal activity is known as

    A. fraud   B. collusion
    C. larceny   D. racketeering

11. A predominant force in modern policing has been the *reform strategy* developed in the latter part of the 20th century. Which of the following has NOT been an element of this strategy?

    A. Ensuring effective discipline and control through elaborate rules and close supervision
    B. Attempting to guarantee the fair and impartial enforcement of the law by insulating the police from close contact with any kind of political influence
    C. Primary reliance on the techniques of random and directed patrol
    D. Emphasizing order maintenance as the primary task of the police

12. What is the term for the legally authorized holding in confinement of a person subject to criminal or juvenile court proceedings, until the point of commitment to a correctional facility or release?

    A. Booking   B. Detention
    C. Arrest   D. Arraignment

13. In what year was the Bill of Rights adopted?

    A. 1776   B. 1789   C. 1791   D. 1801

14. Which of the following constitutional provisions is LEAST likely to apply in state criminal proceedings?   14.____
    A. Protection against cruel and unusual punishment
    B. The requirement that charges on *capital or other infamous crimes* shall be by grand jury indictment
    C. The right against self-incrimination
    D. The right to be tried within the state and district wherein the crime was committed

15. Approximately _____ % of a municipal patrol officer's activities are devoted to criminal law enforcement.   15.____
    A. 10   B. 20   C. 33   D. 75

16. The core function of the entire justice system is typically   16.____
    A. public services   B. order maintenance
    C. crime prevention   D. law enforcement

17. In addition to their other responsibilities, agents of the _____ serve as bailiffs for the federal courts.   17.____
    A. United States Marshal Service
    B. Secret Service
    C. Federal Bureau of Investigation (FBI)
    D. Customs Service

18. Which of the following was an early method of law enforcement that relied on self-help and mutual aid?   18.____
    A. Hue and cry   B. Pennsylvania system
    C. Tithing system   D. Auburn system

19. In some communities, the police take seriously all requests for either law enforcement or order maintenance, but are less likely to respond by making an arrest or otherwise imposing formal sanctions. This type of policing style is usually described as the _____ style.   19.____
    A. service   B. facilitation
    C. legalistic   D. watchman

20. The ancient social order of most human societies can MOST accurately be described as   20.____
    A. loosely organized and sedentary agrarian settlements
    B. small family groups affiliated with tribes or clans
    C. rural settlements administrated from a crude central metropolis
    D. independent, nomadic nuclear families

21. Regardless of location, most county sheriffs in the United States share a set of basic functions. Which of the following is LEAST likely to be included in these?   21.____
    A. Serving civil process on behalf of courts and other agencies
    B. Maintaining county jails
    C. Certifying lists of prospective jurors
    D. Providing bailiff services to county courts

22. Which of the following terms refers specifically to the theft by employees through stealth or deception?

    A. Burglary
    B. Pilferage
    C. Petty larceny
    D. Pillaging

23. To most law enforcement professionals, _____ represents the core of police work.

    A. patrol
    B. deterrence
    C. civil services
    D. investigation

24. Which of the following statements about the early English tithing system is FALSE? It

    A. was most applicable to emergency situations
    B. was of little benefit in unifying the entire nation
    C. tended to conceal crime and perjury in order that individual members of a tithing might not have to make restitution for the acts of another
    D. worked well in an agrarian community where people were content to live in one place

25. The dominant characteristic of the current approach to crime control in the United States is that it

    A. frequently involves force
    B. is first engineered at the grade-school level
    C. is reactive
    D. relies on the idea of rehabilitation

KEY (CORRECT ANSWERS)

1. C
2. A
3. D
4. C
5. C

6. D
7. A
8. A
9. C
10. B

11. D
12. B
13. C
14. B
15. C

16. D
17. A
18. C
19. A
20. B

21. C
22. B
23. A
24. B
25. C

TEST 2

DIRECTIONS: Each question or incomplete statement is followed by several suggested answers or completions. Select the one that BEST answers the question or completes the statement. *PRINT THE LETTER OF THE COREECT ANSWER IN THE SPACE AT THE RIGHT.*

1. The practice of holding dangerous suspects before trial without bail is called   1.____

   A. praxis
   B. preventive detention
   C. discouragement
   D. custodial convenience

2. Which of the following federal agencies is housed in the Department of Justice?   2.____

   A. Bureau of Alcohol, Tobacco and Firearms
   B. Immigration and Naturalization Service (INS)
   C. United States Coast Guard
   D. Secret Service

3. Each of the following is an individual right granted to criminal defendants under the Sixth   3.____
Amendment to the Constitution EXCEPT the right to

   A. have the assistance of legal counsel
   B. confront hostile witnesses
   C. refuse to be witnesses against themselves
   D. be tried by an impartial jury

4. State or federal criminal law statutes are commonly referred to as the   4.____

   A. corpus delectii
   B. tort
   C. penal code
   D. presentment

5. As a reformer of the police profession, William Parker, who became chief of the Los   5.____
Angeles Police Department in 1950, made his greatest contribution to the development
of the profession in the area of

   A. administrative reorganization
   B. clearly defined limits of officer discretion
   C. improved community relations
   D. increased educational requirements for recruits

6. Each of the following is a basic principle of the community policing concept EXCEPT   6.____

   A. emphasizing the response to calls for service
   B. developing closer ties with other government agencies that share responsibilities for community problems
   C. de-emphasizing crime-fighting
   D. concentrating on disorder at the neighborhood level

7. Which of the following types of crimes do NOT contain the need for intent in order to be   7.____
prosecutable?

   A. Strict-liability crimes
   B. Mala prohibitum crimes
   C. Mala in se crimes
   D. Index crimes

5

8. Which of the following time periods corresponds most closely with the period of the Supreme Court's practice of *selective incorporation* of specific individual rights within the meaning of the Fourteenth Amendment?

   A. 1800-1937   B. 1861-1912   C. 1925-1961   D. 1889-1984

9. Under the tithing system of early England, what was the term for the process whereby every able-bodied man had to join in the common chase for offenders?

   A. Borsholder   B. Comes stabuli
   C. Hue and cry   D. Pied poudre

10. In a typical police department, which of the following units would be contained within the administration bureau?

    A. Inspections   B. Records and identification
    C. Data processing   D. Internal investigation

11. What is the term for the official halting or suspension, at any legally prescribed processing point after a recorded justice system entry, of formal criminal or juvenile justice proceedings against an alleged offender—an act typically accompanied by a referral of that person to a treatment or care program administered by a nonjustice or private agency?

    A. Treatment   B. Disposition
    C. Dismissal   D. Diversion

12. Of the following federal law enforcement agencies, which was established most recently?

    A. Drug Enforcement Agency (DEA)
    B. National Park Service
    C. Immigration and Naturalization Service (INS)
    D. Bureau of Alcohol, Tobacco and Firearms (ATF)

13. What is the term for an act committed by a juvenile for which an adult could be prosecuted in a criminal court, but for which a juvenile can be either adjudicated in a juvenile court or prosecuted in a criminal court if the juvenile court transfers jurisdiction?

    A. Diversion   B. Disposition
    C. Misdemeanor   D. Delinquent act

14. The image of the police as *crime fighters* among the media and the public has resulted in a number of serious problems, including
    I. the establishment of an artificial status difference between detectives and patrol officers
    II. the tendency for the public to over-praise police forces in their evaluations
    III. inability for elected officials to make informed decisions about budget priorities
    IV. unrealistic expectations about the ability of the police to prevent crime and catch criminals

    The CORRECT answer is:

    A. I, II, III   B. I, III, IV
    C. I, IV   D. All of the above

15. In which ground-breaking Supreme Court decision was it decided that juvenile defendants were, like adult criminal defendants, entitled to legal counsel in state juvenile court proceedings?

    A. McNabb v. United States (1943)
    B. United States v. Wade (1967)
    C. In re Gault (1967)
    D. Smith v. Wade (1983)

16. Which of the following is a *line* function within a typical police department?

    A. Criminalistics
    B. Prisoner detention
    C. Investigations
    D. Personnel

17. A routine *stop and frisk* is sometimes referred to as a(n)

    A. search and seizure
    B. threshold inquiry
    C. special deterrence
    D. impromptu interrogation

18. The oldest unit of federal law enforcement is the

    A. Federal Bureau of Investigation (FBI)
    B. Immigration and Naturalization Service (INS)
    C. United States Marshal Service
    D. Border Patrol

19. Between 700-900 A.D., Anglo-Saxon England developed precedents for each of the following elements in American law enforcement EXCEPT

    A. fines
    B. capital punishment
    C. involuntary servitude
    D. restitution

20. Most studies on management solutions to police corruption conclude that

    A. strategies aimed at past corruption are more effective than proactive strategies, but only at the level of line officers
    B. for the same corruption control strategy to be effective in police departments of different sizes, the same tactics must be adhered to
    C. strategies aimed at ongoing corruption have the potential to reduce the level of organization of police corruption
    D. administrative actions have little effect on police corruption

21. The recording of an arrest typically includes the identification of the person arrested, the place, the time, the arresting authority, and the reason for the arrest. The police administrative action which includes these elements is known as

    A. booking
    B. indictment
    C. intake
    D. citation

22. Which of the following is a common problem in the organization of police units?

    A. There are often not enough middle managers to oversee the line employees.
    B. Support functions or staff functions are often placed in a single line unit.
    C. Agencies are frequently too decentralized to make unified decisions.
    D. Service and line functions are not adequately delineated.

23. The original, unamended text of the Constitution was limited in its reference to matters of criminal justice. Which of the following were limitations placed on the federal government by this original text?
    I. No deprivation of life, liberty, or property without due process of law
    II. No ex post facto laws, or laws that retroactively
    III. subject citizens to criminal prosecution
    IV. No suspension of the writ of habeas corpus - the writ that protects citizens from imprisonment without trial on specified charges - except in cases of rebellion or invasion that threaten public safety
    V. No bills of attainder, or punishment of citizens by legislative act
    The CORRECT answer is:

    A. I only
    B. I, II, III
    C. II, III, IV
    D. II, IV

24. Which two federal law _____ enforcement agencies work together in the area of smuggling?
    The

    A. Bureau of Alcohol, Tobacco and Firearms (ATF) and the Secret Service
    B. Border Patrol and the Customs Service
    C. Border Patrol and the Secret Service
    D. Secret Service and the Customs Service

25. Which of the following was NOT a general principle included in the original text of the Constitution?

    A. The federal and state governments share equal power within a jurisdiction.
    B. Powers not given to the federal government by the people remain with the states or the people
    C. A republic with popular sovereignty
    D. The separation of powers of the national government into separate branches

KEY (CORRECT ANSWERS)

1. B
2. B
3. C
4. C
5. A

6. A
7. A
8. C
9. C
10. A

11. D
12. A
13. D
14. B
15. C

16. C
17. B
18. C
19. B
20. C

21. A
22. B
23. C
24. B
25. A

EXAMINATION SECTION
TEST 1

DIRECTIONS: Each question or incomplete statement is followed by several suggested answers or completions. Select the one that BEST answers the question or completes the statement. *PRINT THE LETTER OF THE CORRECT ANSWER IN THE SPACE AT THE RIGHT.*

1. For juvenile offenders, the equivalent of adult parole is referred to as   1._____

    A. status parole   B. continuance   C. aftercare   D. probation

2. Which of the following is a document issued by a judicial officer directing that a person who has failed to obey an order or notice to appear be brought before the court?   2._____

    A. Injunction   B. Summons
    C. Bench warrant   D. Search warrant

3. Which of the following is a law enforcement agency within the federal Department of the Interior?   3._____

    A. United States Coast Guard
    B. Bureau of Customs
    C. Bureau of Indian Affairs
    D. Immigration and Naturalization Service (INS)

4. In one of the most significant early Supreme Court rulings on the issue of the national government's powers, the Court of Chief Justice John Marshall reasoned that a power or right not expressly mentioned in the Constitution may be deduced fairly from *more than one of the substantive powers expressly defined, or from them all combined.* What was this court case?   4._____

    A. Marbury v. Madison (1903)   B. McCulloch v. Maryland (1819)
    C. Gibbons v. Ogden (1824)   D. Munn v. Illinois (1877)

5. A set of general legal principles inherited from England, which became precedents for subsequent decisions in American courts, are known collectively as _____ law.   5._____

    A. common   B. tort   C. civil   D. case

6. Which of the following law enforcement developments occurred EARLIEST in England?   6._____

    A. The first police survey
    B. Taxation for police protection
    C. The first detective unit
    D. A system of monetary reward for apprehending bandits and thieves

7. Which of the following is a DISADVANTAGE associated with a decentralized structure in police organizations?   7._____

    A. Generally lower job satisfaction at lower levels
    B. Less timely and more poorly developed operational decisions
    C. Greater need to assure the public that officers' actions are guided by formalized policies and procedures
    D. Preoccupation for higher-level managers on operational matters

8. _____ laws are designed to protect rape victims by prohibiting defense attorneys from inquiring about previous sexual relationships.

    A. Gag B. Sunshine C. Shield D. Blue

9. According to the Police Services Survey, citizens who call police units are most likely to be reporting

    A. noise disturbances
    B. traffic accidents
    C. domestic conflicts
    D. theft

10. Which of the following is credited with taking the first step in developing the community policing approach?

    A. Orlando W. Wilson
    B. August Vollmer
    C. James Q. Wilson
    D. Herman Goldstein

11. If an illegal yet unintended act results from the intent to commit a crime, that act is also considered illegal. This is the principle of

    A. constructive intent
    B. strict liability
    C. transferred intent
    D. mens rea

12. The discretionary police decision to _____ is most likely to affect the official crime rate.

    A. conduct a high-speed pursuit
    B. use physical force
    C. present a case to a prosecutor
    D. patrol an area more aggressively than normal

13. Which of the following Constitutional Amendments represents the first and only time the people have overruled the Supreme Court, establishing their right to the ultimate decision on Constitutional rights?

    A. Eighth
    B. Eleventh
    C. Fourteenth
    D. Seventeenth

14. The 1930s in the United States was a period in which reformers made a concerted effort to redefine the mission of the police. These efforts tended to focus on the mission of

    A. independence from the political process
    B. crime fighting
    C. administrative efficiency
    D. community relations

15. Problem-oriented or community policing can be most accurately described as a _____ process.

    A. planning
    B. triage
    C. proscriptive
    D. centralized

16. When an arrested person is released on recognizance, it is on the condition that he or she

   A. agree to appear for trial at a later date
   B. post a surety amount of the bailment
   C. offer testimony against associated criminal defendants
   D. post the full amount of bail in cash

17. Some law enforcement officers, especially African-American officers, carry the social burden of being both minority-group members as well as members of the law enforcement profession. This situation is known as

   A. estoppel
   B. culture conflict
   C. double marginality
   D. discouragement

18. In which of the following police units is role conflict most likely to become a problem?

   A. Detectives
   B. Patrol
   C. Vice squad
   D. Juvenile units

19. The *spoils era* in American policing, which was marked by gross political interference and corruption in police affairs, lasted roughly from

   A. 1730-1793   B. 1850-1883   C. 1900-1936   D. 1941-1975

20. The main argument against using outcome measures, such as reduced crime, as assessments for the value of police departments is that they

   A. are valuable only to top-level management
   B. are not the best way to represent the value of a police department to the community
   C. present too many difficulties in accurately measuring the police contribution to these results
   D. are not closely audited

21. In the court case of Arizona v. Fulminate (1991), it was ruled that

   A. evidence can be seized without a warrant if it would have been *inevitably discovered by polie officers*
   B. a confession may be used at trial even if police used coercion when it was acquired
   C. for a consent search to be effective the consent must be voluntary, i.e., without threat or coercion
   D. evidence may be admitted to trial even if a search warrant was faulty but police officers acted in *good faith*

22. What is the term for a formal promise not to prosecute in exchange for testimony?

   A. Immunity
   B. Diversion
   C. Waiver
   D. Disposition

23. In which region of the United States do county sheriffs tend to have the most limited role in law enforcement?

   A. West
   B. South
   C. Midwest
   D. Northeast

24. In a typical police department, which of the following units would be contained within the operations bureau?   24._____

    A. Legal adviser
    C. Intelligence
    B. Juvenile
    D. Communications

25. Of all the police functions, which is typically the most demanding in terms of the time and resources of law enforcement agencies?   25._____

    A. Public services
    C. Crime prevention
    B. Order maintenance
    D. Law enforcement

KEY (CORRECT ANSWERS)

1. C
2. C
3. C
4. B
5. A

6. D
7. C
8. C
9. D
10. D

11. C
12. C
13. B
14. B
15. A

16. A
17. C
18. D
19. B
20. C

21. B
22. A
23. D
24. B
25. A

TEST 2

DIRECTIONS: Each question or incomplete statement is followed by several suggested answers or completions. Select the one that BEST answers the question or completes the statement. *PRINT THE LETTER OF THE CORRECT ANSWER IN THE SPACE AT THE RIGHT.*

1. In order to exercise some control over officer discretion, many departments have adopted written rules. The most important disadvantage to this approach is that

   A. officer performance tends to become inconsistent
   B. it encourages disputes about official policy
   C. they do not ensure equal protection
   D. rules cannot be written to cover every possible situation

   1.____

2. What is the term for a criminal defense that maintains the police originated the criminal idea or initiated the criminal action?

   A. Nolo contendere
   B. Entrapment
   C. Illegal search and seizure
   D. Double jeopardy

   2.____

3. The fundamental geographic unit within a police department is typically referred to as the

   A. beat   B. zone   C. precinct   D. sector

   3.____

4. The seeds of the first jury system used in criminal proceedings were found in

   A. Mesopotamia, around 3000 B.C.
   B. Rome, around 1400 B.C.
   C. France, around 785 A.D.
   D. England, around 1600 A.D.

   4.____

5. In the year _____, a Philadelphia ordinance provided for twenty-three policemen to serve by day, and 120 by night, all under a single captain who would be appointed by the mayor.

   A. 1695   B. 1779   C. 1833   D. 1910

   5.____

6. Which of the following is considered to be a primary duty of the federal Drug Enforcement Agency (DEA)?

   A. Regulating the flow and manufacture of legal but controlled drugs
   B. Gathering intelligence on traffickers in illicit drugs
   C. Running drug abuse prevention programs
   D. Enforcing federal laws related to illicit narcotic drugs and cooperating with state and local agencies in the enforcement of state narcotics laws

   6.____

7. The requirement that a search warrant state precisely where the search is to take place and what items are to be seized is the requirement of

   A. particularity   B. locus of control
   C. plain view   D. focal concern

   7.____

8. Which of the following factors is LEAST likely to influence most citizens' fear of crime? 8.____

   A. Garbage on the streets
   B. Noisy teenagers or loiterers
   C. Levels of criminal victimization
   D. Graffiti

9. Which of the following was NOT a development that helped to bring about the great 9.____
   United States police reforms that took place after 1920?

   A. Greater centralization of departments due to the Great Depression
   B. A shift in the American economy toward the production of consumer goods and the migration to metropolitan areas
   C. A redefinition of the police mission as primarily peacekeeping rather than crime fighting
   D. The influence of European achievements on law enforcement

10. Despite the growth of the community policing concept in the United States, it is not with- 10.____
    out its critics. Probably the most important criticism of community policing is that it

    A. is merely an organizational change
    B. does not really permit members of the community to determine the proper police role
    C. contributes to a greater strain in police-community relations
    D. significantly expands police roles and powers within the community

11. Which of the following court cases dealt with the issue of search and seizure? 11.____

    A. Wolf v. Colorado (1949)
    B. Miranda v. Arizona (1966)
    C. Gilbert v. California (1967)
    D. Gardner v. Broderick (1968)

12. Which of the following is NOT a responsibility of the United States Marshal Service? 12.____

    A. Process servers for the federal government
    B. The custody, care, and transport of federal prisoners
    C. Policing illicit drug traffic into the United States
    D. The federal government's witness protection program

13. A court with jurisdiction to try all criminal offenses, including all felonies, and that may or 13.____
    may not hear appeals, is known as a court of _____ jurisdiction.

    A. limited   B. appellate   C. criminal   D. general

14. One characteristic of the military structure used in many police departments is that any 14.____
    one manager or supervisor has a relatively narrow span of control. The purposes of this
    structure include the following EXCEPT

    A. enabling the department to form into operational units of varying size ranging from the individual officer to the entire organization
    B. the elimination of a large corps of middle managers who act as *middlemen* between top management and line officers
    C. ensuring effective discipline and control through very close supervision
    D. pinpointing accountability for command decisions

15. *The right of the people to be secure in their persons, houses, papers, and effects, against unreasonable searches and seizures* is granted by the _____ Amendment to the Constitution.

    A. Third   B. Fourth   C. Sixth   D. Seventh

16. The American Bar Association has identified several individual responsibilities that have been assigned to the police. Which of the following is NOT one of them?
    To

    A. create and maintain a feeling of security in the community
    B. facilitate the movement of people and vehicles
    C. reduce the likelihood of accidents in public places
    D. reduce the opportunities for the commission of crime

17. Law that is enacted by legislative assemblies is known as _____ law.

    A. case
    B. statutory
    C. constitutional
    D. civil

18. What is the term for the misappropriation, misapplication, or illegal disposal of legally entrusted property with intent to defraud the legal owner or intended beneficiary?

    A. Embezzlement
    B. Fraud
    C. Larceny
    D. Extortion

19. Which of the following is not a style of patrol used in most police departments?

    A. Standard
    B. Aggressive
    C. Reactive
    D. Selective

20. Which of the following types of law enforcement units typically has the broadest legislative mandate?

    A. Urban police
    B. Federal agencies
    C. State police
    D. County sheriffs

21. Which of the following police activities is LEAST likely to be sanctioned by public opinion?

    A. Taking suspected law violators into custody
    B. Using force when necessary
    C. Seeking unreported crimes and deterring their commission
    D. Investigating reported crimes

22. Acts that are outlawed because they clash with current norms and public opinions, such as tax, traffic, and drug laws, are known as _____ crimes.

    A. mala in se
    B. venal
    C. mala prohibitum
    D. victimless

23. Which of the following was NOT a finding that led to the development of the community policing movement?

    A. Reducing patrol response time does not increase the probability of arrest
    B. The police spend a majority of their time dealing with crime
    C. Routine patrol is very limited in its ability to deter crime
    D. Most cleared crimes are solved on the basis of information obtained by the first officer to arrive at the scene

24. Which of the following federal law enforcement agencies is responsible for enforcing the Federal Wagering Tax Law?

    A. United States Marshal Service
    B. Bureau of Alcohol, Tobacco and Firearms (ATF)
    C. Secret Service
    D. Internal Revenue Service Intelligence Division

25. Whenever an officer acts on his own initiative or to the extent he can influence the outcome of disorderly situations in which he acts on the initiative of the citizen, a patrol officer is usually expected to take a _____ view of his role.

    A. service
    B. legalistic
    C. discretionary
    D. watchman

KEY (CORRECT ANSWERS)

1. D		11. A	
2. B		12. C	
3. A		13. D	
4. C		14. B	
5. C		15. B	
6. D		16. C	
7. A		17. B	
8. C		18. A	
9. C		19. D	
10. D		20. A	

21. C
22. C
23. B
24. B
25. B

EXAMINATION SECTION
TEST 1

DIRECTIONS: Each question or incomplete statement is followed by several suggested answers or completions. Select the one that BEST answers the question or completes the statement. *PRINT THE LETTER OF THE CORRECT ANSWER IN THE SPACE AT THE RIGHT.*

1. The _____ comprises the earliest known set of codified laws or customs.

    A. Leges Henrici
    B. Assize of Clarendon
    C. Capitularies of Charlemagne
    D. Code of Hammurabi

2. What is the term for a non-jury trial in which a judge hears the trial and renders a verdict?

    A. Affidavit B. Bindover
    C. Bench trial D. Adjudicatory hearing

3. Which of the following is an example of a generalist police force at the state level?

    A. Fish and game wardens B. Investigative departments
    C. Bureau of narcotics D. Highway patrol

4. For an adapted private-sector approach to be successful in the management of a police agency, it must meet certain tests. In this adapted situation, which of the following tests is shared by both public and private sector enterprises?
    I. Operational feasibility and suitability
    II. Legitimacy and support from political and legal officials
    III. Value to the community
    The CORRECT answer is:

    A. I only   B. I, II   C. II, III   D. I, III

5. What is the term for the written order, issued by a law enforcement officer, directing an alleged offender to appear in a specific court at a specified time in order to answer to a criminal charge?

    A. Citation B. Summons
    C. Booking D. Detention

6. The conflict between the crime control and due process models of the criminal process is most likely to be experienced by officers in the _____ unit of a police department.

    A. vice B. criminal investigation
    C. administrative D. patrol

7. The violent behavior that results from the conflict inherent in the drug trade is known as the

    A. short-run hedonism B. stradom formation
    C. systemic link D. transferred intent

8. The team policing experiments of the late 1960s and early 1970s in America are now universally regarded as a failure. Which of the following is not considered to be a reason for this?
They

   A. involved changes in the organizational structure of policing, rather than the nature of basic police services
   B. made middle-man management officers feel threatened
   C. alienated the general public
   D. were poorly planned and executed too hastily

9. What is the term for a written accusation made by a grand jury stemming from its own investigation?

   A. Presentment   B. Information
   C. Subornment   D. Indictment

10. The unlawful taking or attempted taking of property that is in the immediate possession of another, by force or by threat of force, is a crime known as

    A. larceny   B. armed robbery
    C. burglary   D. robbery

11. The police function of crime control tends to be valued most highly by members of the public, who often view other police functions as a dangerous and wasteful distraction. Each of the following is a likely reason for this status EXCEPT

    A. crime control is an urgent and compelling societal task
    B. the police are the organization best suited to dealing with the problem of crime
    C. the proportionally limited resources devoted to crime control in many police organizations
    D. crime control is the function that evokes the greatest enthusiasm and commitment from police themselves

12. Which of the following amendments to the Constitution includes a *due process* clause?

    A. Sixth   B. Eighth
    C. Fourteenth   D. Sixteenth

13. Each of the following is an important drawback associated with the reactive approach to crime control EXCEPT

    A. street offenses are often not dealt with effectively in urban areas because of victims' fears of coming forward
    B. it does not enable the police to prevent specific crimes
    C. it is difficult to deal with so-called victimless crimes
    D. it exercises the maximum amount of state authority over people's lives

14. Orlando Wilson's contributions to the reformation of the American police profession include
    I. upgrading the training of new police recruits
    II. the consolidation of precincts into districts with a clear line of authority
    III. the application of communications technology to police work
    IV. the requirement of two-officer partnerships for each patrolcar

    The CORRECT answer is:

| A. I, III | B. II, IV |
| C. I, II, III | D. All of the above |

15. Most criminal law activity by police involves

    A. violent crime
    B. property crime
    C. public nuisances
    D. dependent persons

16. What is the term for an offense usually punishable by incarceration in a local confinement facility, for a period whose upper limit is prescribed by statute in a given jurisdiction - typically limited to a year or less?

    A. Misdemeanor
    B. Delinquent act
    C. Citation
    D. Felony

17. Which of the following is NOT a problem typically associated with uncontrolled police discretion?

    A. Denial of equal protection
    B. Ineffective personnel supervision
    C. Under-reporting of certain types of crimes
    D. Denial of due process

18. The principles behind the Peelian Reforms, enacted on England's police in 1829, include each of the following EXCEPT

    A. the police should be organized along military lines
    B. the efficiency of police is best proved by the absence of crime
    C. the police must not be under government control
    D. for purposes of public security, every officer must be given a number

19. Of the following factors, which tends to be LEAST important in influencing the behavior of police officers in discretionary situations?

    A. Departmental policy
    B. Characteristics of the individual officer
    C. Situational factors, such as the demeanor of the suspect
    D. Limited police resources

20. Which of the following were precedents established by the Magna Carta of 1215?
    I. The right to avoid self-incrimination
    II. The right of due process
    III. The clear separation of national and local government
    IV. The right of trial by jury

    The CORRECT answer is:

    A. I, II
    B. III, IV
    C. I, III, IV
    D. II, III, IV

21. Of all the executive agencies that act as sources of police functions, probably the most significant is the

    A. prosecutor
    B. police commissioner
    C. mayor
    D. city manager

22. The term *prison* typically refers to a confinement facility having custodial authority over adults sentenced to confinement for a period of more than

    A. six months
    B. one year
    C. three years
    D. five years

23. Which of the following was NOT a typical function of the earliest female police officers in the United States?

    A. Patrol
    B. Vice
    C. Handling female prisoners
    D. Juvenile

24. What is the term for one who is a partner in the commission of a crime?

    A. Confederate
    B. Accessory
    C. Alias
    D. Accomplice

25. Patrol officers make a number of on-the-street discretionary decisions, the most common of which is whether to

    A. stop, question, or frisk a suspect
    B. arrest or write a ticket
    C. use a particular tactic to maintain order
    D. use physical or deadly force

KEY (CORRECT ANSWERS)

1. D	11. C
2. C	12. C
3. D	13. D
4. A	14. C
5. A	15. B
6. B	16. A
7. C	17. C
8. C	18. C
9. A	19. B
10. D	20. D

21. A
22. B
23. A
24. D
25. C

TEST 2

DIRECTIONS: Each question or incomplete statement is followed by several suggested answers or completions. Select the one that BEST answers the question or completes the statement. *PRINT THE LETTER OF THE CORRECT ANSWER IN THE SPACE AT THE RIGHT.*

1. Which of the following is an individual right that is protected under the Eighth Amendment to the Constitution?

    A. The right to legal counsel
    B. The right to a speedy and public trial
    C. The protection against double jeopardy
    D. Protection against excessive bail and excessive fines

    1.____

2. According to the well-known Police Services study, which of the following types of calls to police units is made most frequently?

    A. Requests for information
    B. Reporting nonviolent crimes
    C. Reporting public nuisances
    D. Requests for assistance not related to crime or public order

    2.____

3. An admission of guilt in a criminal case, with the condition that the finding cannot be used against the defendant in any subsequent cases, is referred to as

    A. nolo contendere
    B. respondeat emptor
    C. claiming one's Fifth Amendment right
    D. a guilty plea

    3.____

4. When it occurs, police corruption most commonly takes the form of

    A. internal corruption   B. gratuities
    C. larceny or theft   D. bribes

    4.____

5. Which of the following is a defense to a criminal charge in which the accused maintains he or she lacked the intent to commit the crime?

    A. Entrapment   B. Demeanor
    C. Excuse   D. Ignorance

    5.____

6. In a landmark Supreme Court case, the Court concluded the following: *We hold only that when the process (of interrogating a criminal suspect) shifts from investigatory to accusatory and its purpose is to elicit a confession --our adversary system begins to operate, and, under the circumstances here, the accused must be permitted to consult with his lawyer.*
    In which case was opinion issued?

    A. Mapp v. Ohio (1961)
    B. Gideon v. Wainwright (1963)
    C. Escobedo v. Illinois (1964)
    D. Miranda v. Arizona (1966)

    6.____

7. As law enforcement agencies, beverage or alcohol units are typically operated at the _____ level.

   A. federal   B. state   C. county   D. city

8. What is the term for the intentional causing of the death of another in the legal performance of an official duty or in circumstances defined by law as constituting legal justification?

   A. Voluntary manslaughter
   B. Justifiable homicide
   C. Involuntary manslaughter
   D. Excusable homicide

9. _____ law is made by American judges as they interpret statutory and constitutional provisions in cases coming before them.

   A. Common
   B. Statutory
   C. Case
   D. Constitutional

10. Which of the following court cases most clearly set the earliest and clearest precedent for the exclusionary rule in American criminal justice?

    A. Hurtado v. California (1884)
    B. Mapp v. Ohio (1961)
    C. Berger v. New York (1967)
    D. Benton v. Maryland (1969)

11. Which of the following is NOT a science that is typically incorporated into the field of criminalistics?

    A. Physiology
    B. Pathology
    C. Biology
    D. Chemistry

12. What is the term for a written order issued by a magistrate authorizing and directing that an individual be taken into custody to answer criminal charges?

    A. Writ of habeas corpus
    B. Charge document
    C. Summons
    D. Warrant

13. Only in the broadest sense is the United States federal government involved in the function of order maintenance, and the only agency with any real responsibility in this area is the

    A. Federal Bureau of Investigation (FBI)
    B. Immigration and Naturalization Service (INS)
    C. United States Marshal Service
    D. Central Intelligence Agency (CIA)

14. The first form of municipal police used in America were the _____ formed in Boston in 1636.

    A. day patrols
    B. bay constables
    C. detective corps
    D. night watchmen

15. Which of the following units in a typical police department would be most likely to report directly to the Chief of Police?

    A. Personnel and training
    B. Laboratory
    C. Public information
    D. Community relations

16. American police reforms beginning in the 1930s emphasized the selection and promotion of officers on the basis of *objective* criteria such as tests and personnel rating schemes, rather than on internal political connections. The policeman/scholar who was most clearly responsible for developing this movement was

    A. J. Edgar Hoover
    B. Orlando Wilson
    C. August Vollmer
    D. Samuel Parker

17. Which of the following is a type of specialized law enforcement agency?

    A. Labor bureau
    B. State park ranger/police
    C. Municipal transit police
    D. Alcoholic beverage commission

18. A judicial order requesting that a person detaining another produce the body of the person and give reasons for his capture or detention is called a writ of

    A. corpus delectii
    B. habeas corpus
    C. certiorari
    D. mandamus

19. History has shown that the most immediate effect of creating a civilian oversight mechanism for community police departments is usually a

    A. reform in police personnel practices
    B. dramatic increase in the number of citizen complaints filed
    C. dramatic drop in reported crime
    D. dramatic decrease in the number of citizen complaints filed

20. Before any *custodial interrogation* of a criminal suspect can take place, the suspect must be told that he or she has the right to remain silent, that anything he or she says can and will be used in court, that he or she has the right to an attorney who can be present at any interrogation, and that an attorney will be appointed if the suspect cannot afford one.
    A. The court case that established this protection was

    A. Malloy v. Hogan (1964)
    B. Escobedo v. Illinois (1964)
    C. Miranda v. Arizona (1966)
    D. New York v. Quarles (1984)

21. Which of the following types of law enforcement agencies tends to have the greatest responsibility for civil process?

    A. Urban police
    B. Federal agencies
    C. State police
    D. County sheriffs

22. Violence that is designed to improve the financial or social position of the criminal is described as

    A. peremptory
    B. mercenary
    C. discretionary
    D. instrumental

22._____

23. The original and primary purpose of the _____ is to the enforcement of federal laws related to the counterfeiting of currency, securities, and coin.

    A. Internal Revenue Service Intelligence Division
    B. Customs Service
    C. Secret Service
    D. United States Marshal Service

23._____

24. A crime prevention effort typically has an immediate impact which then dissipates as criminals adjust to new conditions. This phenomenon is known as

    A. extinction
    B. dissipation
    C. impulsivity
    D. discouragement

24._____

25. Law enforcement at the federal level is distinct from that of other levels in that it

    A. tends to avoid the use of plea bargaining in prosecuting offenders
    B. focuses to a greater degree on prevention
    C. issues its field officers from one central source
    D. is almost exclusively specialized in nature

25._____

KEY (CORRECT ANSWERS)

1.	D	11.	C
2.	A	12.	D
3.	A	13.	A
4.	B	14.	D
5.	C	15.	D
6.	C	16.	C
7.	B	17.	D
8.	B	18.	B
9.	C	19.	B
10.	B	20.	C

21. D
22. D
23. C
24. A
25. D

EXAMINATION SECION
TEST 1

DIRECTIONS: Each question or incomplete statement is followed by several suggested answers or completions. Select the one that BEST answers the question or completes the statement. *PRINT THE LETTER OF THE CORRECT ANSWER IN THE SPACE AT THE RIGHT.*

1. Which of the following terms is used to denote the intent or guilty mind that is involved in committing an offense?

    A. Corpus delectii
    B. Mens rea
    C. Voir dire
    D. Actus reus

    1.____

2. Under the tithing system of early England, each tithing was led by a landed proprietor known as a

    A. headborough
    B. thane
    C. reeve
    D. shire-reeve

    2.____

3. Which of the following is NOT typically measured by crime victimization surveys?

    A. Clearance rates
    B. Unreported crime
    C. Citizen attitudes about police
    D. The rate at which people report different crimes

    3.____

4. During what decade did the Supreme Court most clearly begin its movement away from the doctrine of judicial restraint—especially with respect to individual rights?

    A. 1890s   B. 1920s   C. 1950s   D. 1970s

    4.____

5. Which of the following is not typically a form of support given by state police and patrol agencies to local police departments and sheriff's offices?

    A. Criminalistics
    B. Crime prevention
    C. Data processing
    D. Criminal histories

    5.____

6. As a measure of whether a police department provides adequate protection for a community, the police-population ratio suffers from the significant drawback that it

    A. does not take into account the population that is served beyond certain municipal boundaries
    B. fails to differentiate between line and staff positions
    C. does not indicate the actual level of on-the-street police protection
    D. calculates its ratio based only on the population who own property

    6.____

7. According to the UCR, the unlawful taking or attempted taking of property, other than a motor vehicle, from the possession of another is the crime of

    A. burglary   B. robbery   C. pilferage   D. larceny

    7.____

8. The most important factor which shapes – and complicates – the role of police units in the community is their

   A. 24-hour availability
   B. legislative mandates
   C. administrative policies
   D. authority to use force

9. The use of fingerprinting as a means of identification was first developed in

   A. Egypt, around 1800 B.C.
   B. Greece, around 600 B.C.
   C. China, around 500 A.D.
   D. France, around 1870 A.D.

10. A police organization can be said to be organized *programmatically* if

    A. it is divided into the three main bureaus of operations, support, and services
    B. it contains bureaus such as narcotics, robbery, homicide, and sex crimes
    C. it contains bureaus such as administration, patrol, or investigations
    D. work is assigned by area, such as a Main Street Division, Riverside Division, and so on

11. In 1925 the Supreme Court ruled, for the first time, that freedom of speech could be protected against arbitrary state action. The court case which produced this ruling was

    A. Baker v. Carr
    B. Gitlow v. New York
    C. Schenk v. United States
    D. Gregory v. City of Chicago

12. What is the term for the doctrine holding that one's options, decisions, and actions are decided by inherited or environmental causes which act on one's character?

    A. Behaviorism
    B. Positivism
    C. Animism
    D. Determinism

13. Which of the following is an advantage associated with the use of output measures, such as clearances and arrest rates, for assessing the value of a police organization in the community?

    A. They require personnel at all levels to analyze and reflect upon performance.
    B. Their standards are closely and continually audited.
    C. They are easily collected and measured.
    D. They offer a direct method of measuring the value of the police.

14. In the United States, the custom of full police uniforms was first adopted in

    A. Boston in 1654
    B. Philadelphia in 1756
    C. New York in 1856
    D. Chicago in 1911

15. Most police agencies routinely deploy officers on a patrol that can best be described as

    A. conspicuous and irregular
    B. reactive and territorial
    C. modest and unevenly distributed
    D. periodic and aggressive

16. The concept of double jeopardy is provided for in the _____ Amendment to the Constitution.

    A. First B. Fourth C. Fifth D. Eighth

17. Which of the following is an advantage associated with a centralized structure in police organizations?

    A. Public reassurance that the law is applied equally and properly in individual cases
    B. It is in line with the day-to-day work of police officers
    C. It helps to advance the idea of police as professionals
    D. It stresses innovation and problem-solving as a means of getting ahead in the organization

18. Which of the following is a term for a white-collar crime in which a stockbroker makes repeated trades in order to fraudulently increase his or her commission?

    A. Twisting B. Screening C. Churning D. Wracking

19. In police departments where discretion is an issue, the most moderate, and most commonly adopted, strategy for controlling officer discretion is

    A. regulating discretion through written policies
    B. integrated specialized discretion units into training programs
    C. enhancing professional judgment
    D. abolishing discretion

20. Which United States state was the first to employ a form of police at the state level?

    A. New York B. Ohio C. Texas D. Virginia

21. Each of the following is a constitutional provision that has been applied to state criminal proceedings by subsequent Supreme Court rulings EXCEPT

    A. the right to compulsory process for obtaining witnesses in his favor
    B. the protection against being tried twice for the same crime
    C. protection against excessive bail and excessive fines
    D. the right to confront hostile witnesses

22. One legal check on police power that is available to citizens is to file a request for a court order that certain police practices be stopped. Such a court ruling is known as an

    A. enjoinment B. injunction
    C. attainder   D. estoppel

23. What is the term for the conditional freedom granted by a judicial officer to an alleged offender, or an adjudicated adult or juvenile, as long as the person meets certain conditions of behavior?

    A. Suspension B. Parole
    C. Diversion   D. Probation

24. Which of the following federal law enforcement agencies is a bureau of the Immigration and Naturalization Service?

    A. Border Patrol
    B. Bureau of Alcohol, Tobacco and Firearms (ATF)
    C. United States Marshal Service
    D. Customs Service

25. The group called for jury duty, from which jury panels are selected, is the

    A. venire   B. praxis   C. wergild   D. panel

KEY (CORRECT ANSWERS)

1. B
2. B
3. A
4. C
5. B

6. C
7. D
8. A
9. C
10. B

11. B
12. D
13. C
14. C
15. A

16. C
17. A
18. C
19. A
20. C

21. C
22. B
23. D
24. A
25. A

TEST 2

DIRECTIONS: Each question or incomplete statement is followed by several suggested answers or completions. Select the one that BEST answers the question or completes the statement. *PRINT THE LETTER OF THE CORRECT ANSWER IN THE SPACE AT THE RIGHT.*

1. Which of the following is not commonly a source of controversy in police-community relations?

    A. The handling of citizen complaints
    B. Police personnel practices
    C. Policy-making bodies
    D. Police field practices

    1.____

2. The Bertillon System, developed in France in the 1880s, revolutionized law enforcement by establishing

    A. the division of police departments according to different types of crime
    B. the technique of collecting, classifying, and identifying fingerprints
    C. a single central command authority for all municipal police functions
    D. a method for identifying individual criminals by means of their physical characteristics

    2.____

3. Recruitment and selection have proven to be particularly difficult for police departments for several reasons.
Which of the following is NOT one of these reasons?

    A. The bulk of recruitment and selection work is often in the hands of a city or county personnel department
    B. Incorrect assumptions among younger adults about police work, leading to too few candidates in the first place
    C. Police agencies have difficulty identifying the strongest candidates
    D. The police themselves desire an increased entry-level education standard

    3.____

4. Of the ten constitutional amendments included in the Bill of Rights, which are NOT explicitly written as safeguards of personal rights?

    A. Second, Third, and Seventh
    B. Third, Seventh, Ninth, and Tenth
    C. Seventh, Eighth, Ninth, and Tenth
    D. Ninth and Tenth

    4.____

5. The *service* style of policing is most likely to be found in

    A. poor, lower class communities populated by a heterogeneous mix of racial or ethnic minorities, and in which there is a generalized fear of violent crime
    B. large urban areas in which an approach such as community policing is made difficult by the sheer number of citizens
    C. homogeneous middle-class communities where citizens tend to agree on the need for public order
    D. *transitional* communities in which lower-class, high-crime areas border middle-class neighborhoods, creating tension and mistrust

    5.____

33

6. In Griswold v. Connecticut (1965), the Supreme Court

   A. held that though wiretapping was illegal, evidence so obtained could nevertheless be used in a state court
   B. subjected the states to the rule against arbitrary intrusions by the police
   C. ruled that the federal government may abridge an individual's right to free speech only when it creates a *clear and present danger*
   D. used the Ninth Amendment as a basis for a new *right to privacy* and struck down a law that regulated the sale and use of birth control devices

7. The jurisdiction of the Federal Bureau of Investigation typically includes each of the following crimes EXCEPT

   A. violations of citizens' civil rights
   B. espionage by subversive elements
   C. the murder of state, county, or local law enforcement officers
   D. violations of antitrust and bankruptcy laws

8. Which of the following is a court order that requires or commands the performance or cessation of an action?

   A. Writ of certiorari   B. Enjoinment
   C. Affidavit   D. Injunction

9. When probable cause is found to exist at a preliminary hearing, the court orders that the accused be held for trial. This process is known as

   A. summons   B. bindover
   C. booking   D. arraignment

10. In which of the following Supreme Court cases was an exception to the Miranda rule created through the ruling that the police do not need to advise suspects of their constitutional rights when *public safety* is at stake?

    A. Haynes v. Washington (1963)
    B. Escobedo v. Illinois (1964)
    C. Michigan v. Moseley (1975)
    D. New York v. Quarles (1984)

11. Civilian review boards represent a commonly proposed mechanism for improving police accountability, but have often been handicapped by a(n)

    A. narrow focus on incidents of police misconduct
    B. lack of public support
    C. overemphasis on the police functions of order maintenance and public service
    D. lack of understanding when it comes to criminal justice issues

12. The Miranda rule which now applies to all law enforcement officers is an incorporation of elements of the _____ Amendments to the Constitution.

    A. First and Third   B. Third and Fourth
    C. Fifth and Sixth   D. Sixth and Eighth

13. The traditional measure of police success in solving crimes is the 13.____

    A. clearance rate
    B. police-population ratio
    C. accreditation process
    D. Uniform Crime Reports

14. In the process of _____, a person appears before the court in order that the court may inform the individual of the accusation(s) against him or her, and to enter a plea. 14.____

    A. adjudication
    B. indictment
    C. subpoena
    D. arraignment

15. Law enforcement agencies within the United States Treasury Department include each of the following EXCEPT 15.____

    A. United States Marshal Service
    B. Bureau of Customs
    C. Bureau of Alcohol, Tobacco and Firearms (ATF)
    D. Secret Service

16. Which of the following law enforcement concepts was first established by the Statute of Winchester, issued by King Edward of England in 1285? 16.____

    A. Abolition
    B. Deterrence
    C. Curfew
    D. Police patrol

17. Which of the following federal law enforcement agencies is responsible for all federal laws not specifically delegated to some other federal agency? 17.____

    A. Federal Bureau of Investigation (FBI)
    B. United States Marshal Service
    C. Secret Service
    D. Internal Revenue Service Intelligence Division

18. What is the term for the lawful authority of a court or administrative agency to hear or act upon a case from its beginning, and to pass judgment on it? 18.____

    A. General jurisdiction
    B. Predisposition
    C. Original jurisdiction
    D. Eminent domain

19. Over the years, public opinion studies concerning people's attitudes toward police have revealed each of the following EXCEPT 19.____

    A. racial minorities consistently rate the police less favorably than whites
    B. people generally rate the police less favorably than most other professions
    C. public attitudes toward police are remarkably stable over time
    D. the most commonly expressed dissatisfaction with police performance is a desire for more police protection

20. Which of the following is NOT an individual right granted under the Fifth Amendment to the Constitution? 20.____
    The

    A. protection against cruel and unusual punishment
    B. right against self-incrimination
    C. protection against being imprisoned without due process of law
    D. protection against being tried twice for the same crime

21. What is the term for the taking of the possessions of another through deception or cheating?   21._____

    A. Petty larceny   B. Fraud
    C. Burglary   D. Robbery

22. Most patrol officers report that the most commonly used method for maintaining order in a public place is   22._____

    A. requesting
    B. reasoning
    C. ordering
    D. the use of the body without touching

23. The finding of criminal liability for an unintentional act that is the result of negligence or recklessness is termed   23._____

    A. opportunism   B. constructive intent
    C. informed consent   D. mens rea

24. Which of the following units in a typical police department would be contained within the services bureau?   24._____

    A. Traffic
    B. Planning, research, and analyses
    C. Community relations
    D. Records and identification?

25. A person commits sexual intercourse with a female legally of the age of consent, but who is unconscious. The person would most likely be charged with   25._____

    A. rape without force or consent
    B. forcible rape
    C. sexual assault
    D. statutory rape

KEY (CORRECT ANSWERS)

1. C
2. D
3. B
4. D
5. C

6. D
7. C
8. B
9. B
10. D

11. A
12. C
13. A
14. D
15. A

16. C
17. B
18. C
19. B
20. A

21. B
22. C
23. B
24. D
25. A

EXAMINATION SECTION
TEST 1

DIRECTIONS: Each question or incomplete statement is followed by several suggested answers or completions. Select the one that BEST answers the question or completes the statement. *PRINT THE LETTER OF THE CORRECT ANSWER IN THE SPACE AT THE RIGHT.*

1. The UNIFORM CRIME REPORTS

    A. take serious note of criminals' social class
    B. take no note of criminals' social class
    C. occasionally record class backgrounds
    D. purposely avoid recording class backgrounds
    E. assume a classless society

2. The concept of "categoric risks," attributed to sociologist Walter Reckless, refers to the
    I. greater likelihood of lower class people to be arrested
    II. greater likelihood of upper class people to be arrested
    III. lack of legal protections in some classes of society
    IV. tendency of judges to be lenient with white people
    V. tendency of rich people to bribe judges

    The CORRECT answer is:

    A. I *only*   B. I, III
    C. II *only*   D. II, IV, V
    E. none of the above

3. The President's Commission on Law Enforcement and Administration of Justice found that, as of 1979, UNIFORM CRIME REPORTS

    A. accurately estimate crime
    B. underestimate crime by half
    C. underestimate crime several times
    D. overestimate crimes
    E. are statistically biased

4. A MAJOR source of criminology data comes from the

    A. LEAA   B. NORC   C. UCR   D. FBI   E. CIA

5. The PRIMARY founders of the classical school of criminology were
    I. Oliver Wendell Holmes
    II. Cesar Beccaria
    III. Jeremy Bentham
    IV. Cesare Lombroso
    V. C. Wright Mills

    The CORRECT answer is:

    A. I, II, IV   B. I, V
    C. II, III   D. II, IV
    E. III, IV, V

6. Criminologists who explain criminal behavior WITHOUT referring to biological models *usually* refer to
    I. interpersonal relations
    II. socialization
    III. chromosomal variations
    IV. police records
    V. personal experience
   The CORRECT answer is:

   A. I *only*
   B. I, II
   C. III *only*
   D. II, III
   E. IV, V

7. Research shows that
    I. crime and psychological disorders are associated
    II. crime and psychological disorders are not associated
    III. relatively few prisoners are psychotic
    IV. 5% or less of convicted prisoners are psychotic
    V. sane people rarely commit crimes
   The CORRECT answer is:

   A. I *only*
   B. I, V
   C. II, III
   D. II, III, IV
   E. IV, V

8. Psychologists and sociologists researching crime disagree *primarily* on

   A. whether there are criminal personality types
   B. whether statistics can accurately represent real crime
   C. methodological flaws in data collection
   D. interpretation of data
   E. how criminology ought to be taught in college

9. Howard Becker was responsible for popularizing the criminological theory of

   A. labeling
   B. differential association
   C. theory of anomie
   D. subcultural theories
   E. positive reinforcement

10. One can characterize labeling theory informally by saying that
    I. people become criminals by imitating people around them
    II. people tend to fulfill others' expectations of them
    III. social scientists should not label people
    IV. scientific classification helps explain behavior
    V. crime becomes a "self-fulfilling prophecy"
   The CORRECT answer is:

   A. I *only*
   B. II, V
   C. III, IV
   D. IV
   E. V *only*

11. A *primary* concept connected with labeling theory is

    A. deviance
    B. punishment
    C. classification
    D. ostracism
    E. stereotypes

12. Professor Edwin Sutherland developed the criminological theory of

    A. labeling
    B. differential association
    C. theory of anomie
    D. subcultural theories
    E. positive reinforcement

13. Emile Durkheim developed the criminological theory of

    A. labeling
    B. differential association
    C. theory of anomie
    D. subcultural theories
    E. positive reinforcement

14. The Code of Hammurabi is
    I. a relatively recent sociological phenomenon
    II. traceable to ancient times
    III. identifiable with lex taliones
    IV. an enlightened code
    V. currently popular

    The CORRECT answer is:

    A. I *only*
    B. I, IV
    C. II *only*
    D. II, III
    E. III, V

15. A *primary* concept in the Hammurabi code is
    I. turning the other cheek to attackers
    II. wreaking revenge on criminals
    III. an eye for an eye
    IV. punishing criminals the way they harmed victims
    V. reform

    The CORRECT answer is:

    A. I *only*
    B. I, V
    C. II, III
    D. II, III, IV
    E. III, IV, V

16. Albert Cohen, besides being noted for his research on juvenile delinquency, is largely responsible for the criminological theory of

    A. labeling
    B. differential association
    C. theory of anomie
    D. subcultural theories
    E. positive reinforcement

17. The criminal phenomenon *most aptly* explained by differential association theory is

    A. assault and battery
    B. white collar crime
    C. theft
    D. murder
    E. psychopathic homicide

18. Differential association occurs *primarily* through

    A. media images
    B. affective deviations
    C. intimate groups
    D. role models
    E. economic privation

19. White collar crime includes
    I. false advertising
    II. kickbacks for political favors
    III. fee splitting
    IV. padding expense accounts
    V. lying to the IRS

    The CORRECT answer is:

    A. I, III, IV
    B. II, III
    C. II, III, IV, V
    D. III, IV
    E. all of the above

20. Prosecuting white collar crimes is difficult because
    I. offenders are not often apprehended
    II. offenders have high social status
    III. administrative courts are used rather than criminal courts
    IV. corporations bribe judges
    V. no harm results from white collar crime

    The CORRECT answer is:

    A. I only
    B. I, II, V
    C. II, III
    D. II, III, IV
    E. all of the above

21. Contemporary versions of differential association theory emphasize the psychological theories of
    I. Freudian psychoanalysis
    II. behaviorism
    III. operant conditioning
    IV. group therapy
    V. Gestalt psychology

    The CORRECT answer is:

    A. I only
    B. II only
    C. II, III
    D. IV, V
    E. all of the above

22. One fact that refutes differential association explanations of criminal behavior is that
    I. some individuals use legitimate business skills to commit crimes
    II. some who are conditioned still do not commit crimes
    III. they are formulated too abstractly
    IV. they are difficult to test mathematically
    V. they cannot predict criminal behavior

    The CORRECT answer is:

    A. I only
    B. I, II, V
    C. II, III, IV
    D. IV only
    E. all of the above

23. The concept of *anomie* means

    A. isolation
    B. loneliness
    C. anonymity
    D. normlessness
    E. deviant

24. Durkheim used the concept of anomie *primarily* to explain

    A. white collar crime
    B. violent crimes
    C. suicide
    D. murder
    E. mass murders

25. Anomie is the result of
    I. divorced families
    II. the lack of integration between goals
    III. the lack of legitimate means to attain goals
    IV. the presence of examples of illegitimate goal-achievement
    V. child abuse

    The CORRECT answer is:

    A. I *only*
    B. I, II
    C. II, III
    D. III *only*
    E. IV, V

26. A good synonym for the criminological term *anomie* is

    A. isolation
    B. discouragement
    C. alienation
    D. ostracism
    E. psychopathology

27. Groups exhibiting behavior associated with anomie are
    I. revolutionary groups
    II. paranoid schizophrenics
    III. suicidal people
    IV. slum dwellers
    V. neurotics

    The CORRECT answer is:

    A. I, III
    B. II, III
    C. II, III, IV
    D. III, V
    E. IV *only*

28. The innovative person who is anomie is one who

    A. rejects the goals, but not the means, of social success
    B. rejects the means, but not the goals, of social success
    C. creates the scheme of a new social order
    D. creates his own, better world
    E. rejects materialism for asceticism

29. Anomie is a useful concept for explaining contemporary crimes of

    A. violence
    B. a white-collar nature
    C. property
    D. aggravated assault
    E. passion

30. Subcultural theories of crime causation stress that
    I. subcultures have deviant norms
    II. subcultures are economically depressed
    III. individual behavior reflects group dynamics
    IV. most crime is committed in subcultures
    V. crimes can be avoided by avoiding subcultures
    The CORRECT answer is:

    A. I only
    B. I, III
    C. II, V
    D. III only
    E. IV, V

31. Members of gangs in the working class do NOT exhibit the middle class characteristics and goals of
    I. suppression of aggression
    II. acquisitiveness
    III. self-reliance
    IV. ambition
    V. projection
    The CORRECT answer is:

    A. I only
    B. I, II, V
    C. II only
    D. II, III
    E. II, III, IV

32. Critics of subcultural theories claim that delinquent gang members
    I. are ambivalent toward middle class goals
    II. act out sublimal fantasies
    III. are victims of social environments
    IV. neutralize and rationalize their actions
    V. become civic leaders later in life
    The CORRECT answer is:

    A. I only
    B. I, II
    C. I, IV
    D. III, IV
    E. II, V

33. Types of subcultures of interest to criminologists include _____ subcultures.
    I. criminal
    II. anomic
    III. conflict
    IV. retreatist
    V. Utopian
    The CORRECT answer is:

    A. I, II
    B. I, III
    C. I, III, IV
    D. II, III, V
    E. III, IV, V

34. Criminal subcultures DIFFER from conflict subcultures in that the former
    I. channel aggression and the latter do not
    II. have role models and the latter do not
    III. are likely to be arrested and the latter are not
    IV. are less likely to engage in gang fights
    V. produce more professional criminals
    The CORRECT answer is:

    A. I only
    B. I, III
    C. II only
    D. II, IV, V
    E. IV, V

35. Penal reform theories rely upon the fundamental claim that
    I. offenders ought to be punished
    II. criminals deserve to be paid back for harm they inflict
    III. penal institutions ought to protect society
    IV. punishment ought to deter crime
    V. prisons ought not to produce worse criminals
    The CORRECT answer is:

    A. I only
    B. I, III
    C. II only
    D. II, III, IV
    E. III, IV, V

36. American Quakers contributed to prison reform by
    I. advocating reforming offenders
    II. discouraging imprisonment
    III. encouraging imprisonment
    IV. supporting rehabilitation
    V. advocating religious conversion
    The CORRECT answer is:

    A. I only
    B. I, III
    C. I, III, IV
    D. II, IV, V
    E. III, V

37. A fundamental concept of American penology, as a result of the Quaker influence, is

    A. revenge
    B. retribution
    C. shame
    D. penitence
    E. pacifism

38. The origin of the word "penitentiary" for prison can be explained by referring to
    I. the idea that offenders should be penitent
    II. the encouragement for prisoners to learn a trade
    III. ancient legal customs of punishment
    IV. lex taliones
    V. English common law
    The CORRECT answer is:

    A. I only
    B. I, II, V
    C. II only
    D. III only
    E. III, IV, V

39. A MAJOR drawback of the Quaker approach to penology was that of

   A. problems prisoners had in groups while incarcerated
   B. offenders who learned new criminal techniques in prison
   C. too much solitary confinement of prisoners
   D. too much reliance on private charity for expenses
   E. offenders refusing to become religious converts

40. A popular administrative plan for penal institutions still in use is called the
   I. silent system
   II. Auburn plan
   III. solitary system
   IV. interactionist plan
   V. cost efficient plan

   The CORRECT answer is:

   A. I only
   B. I, II
   C. II only
   D. II, IV
   E. III, V

41. Factor(s) that *largely* refute(s) the deterrent effects of capital punishment is(are)
   I. the similarity of murder rates in states both lacking and maintaining capital punishment
   II. the difference in homicide rates between states with and without capital punishment
   III. that no one knows how to completely stop homicide
   IV. that mostly lovers and relatives murder each other
   V. that there will always be murderers

   The CORRECT answer is:

   A. I, V
   B. II only
   C. III, IV
   D. III, V
   E. IV only

42. Probation consists *primarily* of
   I. the suspension of a sentence
   II. the elimination of a sentence
   III. leniency given because of good behavior
   IV. rewarding compliant prisoners
   V. reducing sentences

   The CORRECT answer is:

   A. I only
   B. I, III
   C. II only
   D. II, III, V
   E. IV only

43. The origins of American probation in penology are

   A. traceable to rehabilitation theory
   B. largely the result of Bentham's theory
   C. in the tradition of English common law
   D. based on American Puritanism
   E. contrary to English common law

44. Parole DIFFERS from probation in that the
    I. former involves incarcerated prisoners
    II. latter involves incarcerated prisoners
    III. former results from criminal, not administrative, courts
    IV. latter results from criminal, not administrative, courts
    V. former is more humane than the latter
    The CORRECT answer is:

    A. I *only*
    B. I, IV
    C. II *only*
    D. III, V
    E. IV, V

45. Currently, prisoners who are released from penal institutions are

    A. released automatically
    B. released long after they are due
    C. released on parole
    D. put on probation
    E. reformed

46. *Disengagement* is a term used by criminologists to refer to processes
    I. resulting in isolation
    II. designed to reduce the number of relationships
    III. resulting in immersion in a social role
    IV. resulting in separation from social roles
    V. in which criminals rationalize their actions
    The CORRECT answer is:

    A. I *only*
    B. I, II, V
    C. II *only*
    D. II, III, V
    E. II, IV

47. Continuity theory is an important factor in explaining
    I. adolescent behavior
    II. behavior studied by gerontologists
    III. why people perpetuate habits
    IV. why people become innovative
    V. aberrant behavior
    The CORRECT answer is:

    A. I *only*
    B. I, III, V
    C. II *only*
    D. II, III
    E. IV *only*

48. Offenders convicted of crimes ought to be
    I. incarcerated in local jails
    II. incarcerated in prisons
    III. protected from mass murderers
    IV. granted medical care
    V. shot at dawn
    The CORRECT answer is:

    A. I *only*
    B. II *only*
    C. II, III
    D. II, IV
    E. V *only*

49. One of the *fundamental* concepts of American criminal procedures is
    I. due process
    II. administrative efficiency
    III. rex taliones
    IV. presumption of innocence
    V. experts' opinions

    The CORRECT answer is:

    A. I *only*
    B. I, II
    C. I, IV
    D. III
    E. IV, V

50. A concept originating in Roman law and affecting American criminal legislation based on English common law is

    A. nonage
    B. tort
    C. death penalty
    D. discretion
    E. probation

KEY (CORRECT ANSWERS)

1. B	11. A	21. C	31. E	41. A
2. B	12. B	22. E	32. C	42. B
3. C	13. C	23. D	33. C	43. C
4. A	14. D	24. C	34. D	44. B
5. C	15. D	25. C	35. E	45. C
6. B	16. D	26. C	36. C	46. E
7. D	17. B	27. A	37. D	47. D
8. A	18. C	28. B	38. A	48. D
9. A	19. E	29. C	39. C	49. C
10. B	20. C	30. B	40. B	50. A

EXAMINATION SECTION
TEST 1

DIRECTIONS: Each question or incomplete statement is followed by several suggested answers or completions. Select the one that BEST answers the question or completes the statement. *PRINT THE LETTER OF THE CORRECT ANSWER IN THE SPACE AT THE RIGHT.*

1. The age group *most* responsible for violent crimes against the person is(are):
    I. 14-18
    II. 18-24
    III. 24-29
    IV. 29-35
    V. 35-45
    The CORRECT answer is:

    A. I *only*
    B. II *only*
    C. III, IV
    D. V *only*
    E. I, II

2. MOST violent crimes are
    I. inter-racial
    II. intra-racial
    III. committed by men
    IV. committed by women
    V. solved by arrest
    The CORRECT answer is:

    A. I *only*
    B. II *only*
    C. I, III
    D. II, V
    E. I, IV

3. Social scientific methods were *first* used to study suicide by the sociologist(s)
    I. H. L. A. Hart
    II. Weber
    III. Durkheim
    IV. Riesman
    V. Oliver Wendell Holmes
    The CORRECT answer is:

    A. I, IV
    B. II, V
    C. III *only*
    D. IV *only*
    E. none of the above

4. Social scientists have shown that deviance is
    I. inherent in certain forms of behavior
    II. conferred upon certain forms of behavior by societies
    III. a normal result of stable institutions
    IV. an abnormal reaction against stable institutions
    V. normal
    The CORRECT answer is:

A. I only B. II only
C. I, IV D. II, III
E. IV, V

5. Crimes in which there is a *high* probability that the offender and victim were already acquainted with each other include
   I. auto theft
   II. burglary
   III. rape
   IV. murder
   V. embezzlement
   The CORRECT answer is:

   A. I *only* B. I, II
   C. III, V D. IV *only*
   E. III, IV

6. MOST crimes against the person are committed
   I. at home
   II. near one's place of residence
   III. while traveling in unfamiliar places
   IV. because of alcoholism
   V. on the street
   The CORRECT answer is:

   A. I, IV B. II *only*
   C. III *only* D. III, IV
   E. IV, V

7. In the United States, the group *most likely* to be victims of crime are
   I. teenagers
   II. women
   III. black men
   IV. black women
   V. children
   The CORRECT answer is:

   A. I *only* B. I, II, V
   C. II, IV, V D. III, IV
   E. III *only*

8. The country which has the LARGEST proportion of criminal homicides is

   A. Canada B. Great Britain
   C. United States D. Denmark
   E. Sweden

9. According to Interpol, a MAJOR area of crime increase is

   A. aggravated assault B. unjustified homicide
   C. bribery D. theft
   E. none of the above

10. *Ideally,* punishment should be

    I. effective
    II. justified
    III. painless
    IV. inexpensive
    V. discreet

    The CORRECT answer is:

    A. I *only*
    B. I, II
    C. III, IV
    D. III, IV, V
    E. all of the above

11. An increasingly important tool in criminal justice administration is the

    I. psychiatric social worker
    II. intelligence test
    III. personality profile
    IV. cost-benefit analysis
    V. computer

    The CORRECT answer is:

    A. I *only*
    B. I, III
    C. V *only*
    D. IV, V
    E. I, II, III

12. The view holding that human behavior can be scientifically analyzed into causes and effects is called

    A. retributionism
    B. rehabilitationism
    C. psychological determinism
    D. natural law theory
    E. none of the above

13. Both the United States and Canadian legal systems include

    I. writs of assistance
    II. magistrates
    III. traditions from English common law
    IV. the same criminal code
    V. the right of individuals to sue companies

    The CORRECT answer is:

    A. I, II
    B. I, III, V
    C. II *only*
    D. II, III
    E. III, IV, V

14. The U.S. President's Commission on Law Enforcement and the Administration of Justice Task Force reported that

    I. arrest records are incomplete
    II. mathematically, 40% of male U.S. children will be arrested for a non-traffic offense
    III. police and correctional offices have different approaches
    IV. mathematical approaches to crime causation are deficient
    V. crime is clearly decreasing

    The CORRECT answer is:

A. I *only*   B. II, III
C. III, IV   D. III, IV, V
E. all of the above

15. The study of *criminal recidivism* includes
    I. penology
    II. sociology
    III. psychology
    IV. jurisprudence
    V. philosophy
    The CORRECT answer is:

    A. I *only*   B. I, II, V
    C. III, IV   D. IV *only*
    E. all of the above

16. *Penology* is the study of
    I. criminals
    II. offenses
    III. prisons
    IV. crime statistics
    V. deviant behavior
    The CORRECT answer is:

    A. I *only*   B. I, II, III, V
    C. III *only*   D. III, IV
    E. all of the above

17. For criminological purposes, a *social problem* is

    A. whatever members of the criminal justice system think it is
    B. a condition which a large number of people believe to be a deviation from a valued norm
    C. any instance in which someone is harmed or hurt
    D. any instance in which there is a financial loss
    E. all of the above

18. The difference between a *subjective* and *objective* social problem, for criminologists, can BEST be characterized as
    I. personal vs. scientific
    II. objective problems are publicly verifiable
    III. problems that are relatively free of controversy are objective
    IV. problems that are idiosyncratic are subjective
    V. quantifiable vs. not quantifiable
    The CORRECT answer is:

    A. I *only*   B. II, III
    C. II, III, IV   D. IV *only*
    E. II, III, IV, V

19. Mass communications have influenced crime in that
    I. televisions are hot items for thieves
    II. people are aware of their relative deprivation
    III. criminals use techniques seen on television to commit crimes
    IV. apprehending criminals is much easier now
    V. criminal behavior has high publicity
    The CORRECT answer is:

    A. I, II
    B. I, III, V
    C. II *only*
    D. II, III, IV
    E. all of the above

20. According to Weber, power can be characterized as
    I. people realizing their own will against others' resistance
    II. people using extreme means to achieve an end
    III. wanting high prestige and social position
    IV. the achievement of self-sufficiency
    V. economic stability
    The CORRECT answer is:

    A. I *only*
    B. II *only*
    C. II, III, IV
    D. III, V
    E. IV *only*

21. One aspect of crime control and prevention *frequently* emphasized by sociologists is the

    A. influence of drugs and alcohol on crime
    B. class structure of society
    C. probable hidden motives of offenders
    D. total costs to the taxpayer of crime control
    E. none of the above

22. The term *"social norms"* refers to
    I. rules set up by prominent society members
    II. norms of conduct specifying what people ought to do
    III. norms of conduct predicting what people actually do
    IV. behavioral criteria that are normative
    V. statistical profiles of human behavior
    The CORRECT answer is:

    A. I, III, V
    B. II *only*
    C. II, III
    D. II, IV
    E. IV, V

23. A crucial concept in the social sciences is *"socialization,* which is the process
    I. of training children in a language
    II. of learning to get along with peers
    III. of learning to manipulate society
    IV. children undergo in learning social values
    V. of indoctrination
    The CORRECT answer is:

A. I, II B. I, III, V
C. II *only* D. III, IV, V
E. IV *only*

24. If a law is repealed, the chances are that
    I. it was a bad law
    II. it was an unpopular law
    III. it ceased to reflect people's values
    IV. someone paid for it to be changed
    V. it was unenforceable
    The CORRECT answer is:

    A. I, III B. II *only*
    C. III, V D. IV, V
    E. all of the above

25. Two constitutional guarantees that *frequently* impede the judicial process are those of

    A. freedom of speech and the right to assemble
    B. the right to assemble and due process
    C. due process and the right to a speedy trial
    D. the right to a speedy trial and the right to legal defense
    E. none of the above

26. "Legal paternalism" refers to the view that claims that
    I. the law ought to improve people
    II. laws should respect privacy
    III. laws should restrain people for their own good
    IV. laws should reflect the will of the people
    V. laws regulate social stability
    The CORRECT answer is:

    A. I *only* B. I, III
    C. II *only* D. II, IV, V
    E. III, V

27. The *organic* view of society maintains that
    I. individuals are the basic component of society
    II. groups are the basic component of society
    III. society is in constant flux and change
    IV. society can be quantitatively analyzed
    V. biological causes best account for crime
    The CORRECT answer is:

    A. I *only* B. II *only*
    C. II, III D. III, IV, V
    E. III, V

28. The *atomic* view of society maintains that
    I. individuals are the basic component of society
    II. groups are the basic component of society
    III. society is in constant flux and change
    IV. society can be quantitatively analyzed
    V. various parts of society influence each other
    The CORRECT answer is:

A. I *only* B. I, IV
C. II *only* D. II, III, V
E. V *only*

29. The difference between *ascribed* status and *achieved* status is that the   29._____

    A. former can be falsified
    B. latter can be falsified
    C. former is given, the latter made
    D. former is more valuable than the latter
    E. none of the above

30. Our right to freedom of movement can be outweighed by   30._____
    I. having smallpox
    II. committing a crime
    III. others' right to the same
    IV. laws against vagrancy
    V. endangering others
    The CORRECT answer is:

    A. I, II B. I, II, III
    C. III, IV D. III, IV, V
    E. all of the above

31. The Prohibition Laws of the 20's and 30's are an example of   31._____
    I. ineffective legislation
    II. paternalistic law
    III. retributionism
    IV. general prevention
    V. positivism
    The CORRECT answer is:

    A. I *only* B. I, II, V
    C. II *only* D. III, IV
    E. III, IV, V

32. One factor heavily influencing criminology theories is   32._____
    I. ideology
    II. academic institutions
    III. quantitative methods
    IV. moral beliefs
    V. scientific verification
    The CORRECT answer is:

    A. I *only* B. I, II
    C. I, IV D. II, III, IV
    E. V *only*

33. The concept of "overcriminalization" refers to the view that criminals   33._____

    A. are genetically deviant
    B. know right from wrong
    C. are perfectable
    D. are harassed by legal procedure
    E. commit too many crimes

34. Representatives of the criminal justice system came under attack after the 1960's because
    I.   many people considered the law unresponsive
    II. people began to complain of courtroom delays and racism
    III. the law was perceived to protect only the wealthy
    IV. the police hated hippies
    V.   they had bad publicity
   The CORRECT answer is:

   A. I only
   B. I, II, III
   C. II only
   D. III, IV
   E. IV, V

35. Criminological research focuses upon
    I.   kinds of people
    II. kinds of environment
    III. power and conflict
    IV. kinds of laws
    V.   subliminal motivation
   The CORRECT answer is:

   A. I only
   B. I, II
   C. I, II, III
   D. II, IV, V
   E. III, IV, V

36. *Positivism* seriously influenced criminology in that it
    I.   denied free will
    II. separated morality from law
    III. rejected negative thinking
    IV. considered science as a model
    V.   invalidated previous models
   The CORRECT answer is:

   A. I only
   B. I, II, IV
   C. III only
   D. IV, V
   E. all of the above

37. The origin of prison work-houses is attributable to
    I.   the results of cost-benefit analyses
    II. the Protestant work ethic
    III. the belief that hard work is morally edifying
    IV. the desire to see criminals suffer
    V.   philanthropic efforts
   The CORRECT answer is:

   A. I only
   B. I, IV, V
   C. II only
   D. II, III, IV
   E. all of the above

38. The "medical model" of criminology assumes that
    I. doctors know more about people than lawyers
    II. crime is an illness that can be cured
    III. there are biological causes for criminal behavior
    IV. crime is NOT a social reaction to the environment
    V. people make rational decisions
    The CORRECT answer is:

    A. I *only*
    B. I, III
    C. II, III
    D. II, III, IV
    E. III, IV, V

39. The "environmental model" of criminology assumes that
    I. environmental factors can cause crime
    II. people adapt to environments to survive
    III. crime can be socially adaptive
    IV. individual therapy can be an effective crime deterrent
    V. biological factors contribute to criminal behavior
    The CORRECT answer is:

    A. I *only*
    B. I, II
    C. I, II, III
    D. II, IV, V
    E. all of the above

40. Environmental criminologists believe that
    I. only individuals can be pathological
    II. societies can be pathological
    III. criminal behavior is rational
    IV. criminal behavior is irrational
    V. psychological analysis is crucial
    The CORRECT answer is:

    A. I *only*
    B. I, IV, V
    C. II *only*
    D. II, III
    E. III, V

41. *"Mens rea"* refers to
    I. male offenders
    II. mental items
    III. motives
    IV. passion and premeditation
    V. cyclical activities
    The CORRECT answer is:

    A. I *only*
    B. II *only*
    C. II, III, IV
    D. II, III, V
    E. II *only*

42. The reason we do NOT perform public drawing and quartering of mass murderers is that it

    A. is very sloppy
    B. would provide people with gruesome pleasure
    C. is cruel and inhumane punishment

D. is cruel and unusual punishment
E. all of the above

43. MOST criminologists view the state as
    I. the source of all problems in law enforcement
    II. the source of law
    III. a neutral entity with respect to crime
    IV. largely uninvolved with the criminal justice system
    V. unavoidable and unfortunate
    The CORRECT answer is:

    A. I, IV, V
    B. II only
    C. II, III, V
    D. III only
    E. III, IV

43.____

44. Recent criminology theory views the state as
    I. a nuisance
    II. the source of law
    III. politically involved with criminal justice administration
    IV. a non-neutral power
    V. a neutral power
    The CORRECT answer is:

    A. I, V
    B. II only
    C. II, III, V
    D. III only
    E. III, IV

44.____

45. A topic much discussed in the history of philosophy and of relevance to criminology is that of
    I. psychological determinism
    II. free will and determinism
    III. morality and the law
    IV. paternalism
    V. pathology
    The CORRECT answer is:

    A. I, IV
    B. II only
    C. II, IV
    D. III, V
    E. all of the above

45.____

46. One factor difficult for criminologists to evaluate is
    I. motives
    II. intentions
    III. the purpose of the law
    IV. court procedures
    V. prison statistics
    The CORRECT answer is:

    A. I only
    B. I, II
    C. III only
    D. III, IV, V
    E. IV, V

46.____

47. A 19th century theory of criminology was

    A. positivism
    B. natural law
    C. phrenology
    D. cybernetics
    E. none of the above

48. The study of *phrenology* concerned
    I. biological Darwinism
    II. head shapes
    III. genes
    IV. environmental influences
    V. behavior modification

    The CORRECT answer is:

    A. I *only*
    B. I, II, III
    C. II *only*
    D. II, III, V
    E. IV, V

49. The *primary* contention of phrenologists was that

    A. only those who adapted, perhaps using crime, survived
    B. head shape determines the functions of one's brain
    C. criminal behavior is built into our genetic code
    D. environments influence criminals more than anything else
    E. none of the above

50. Geneticists in criminology claim that

    A. head shapes determine brain functions
    B. environments shape criminal behavior
    C. chromosomes determine violent behavior
    D. humans have free will
    E. all of the above

KEY (CORRECT ANSWERS)

1. B	11. D	21. B	31. C	41. C
2. C	12. C	22. D	32. C	42. D
3. C	13. D	23. E	33. C	43. E
4. D	14. E	24. C	34. B	44. E
5. E	15. A	25. C	35. C	45. C
6. B	16. C	26. B	36. B	46. B
7. D	17. B	27. C	37. C	47. C
8. C	18. E	28. B	38. D	48. C
9. D	19. D	29. C	39. C	49. B
10. B	20. A	30. E	40. D	50. D

EXAMINATION SECTION
TEST 1

DIRECTIONS: Each question or incomplete statement is followed by several suggested answers or completions. Select the one that BEST answers the question or completes the statement. *PRINT THE LETTER OF THE CORRECT ANSWER IN THE SPACE AT THE RIGHT.*

1. Methods of crime control include:
    I. Reformation and treatment
    II. Deterrence
    III. Incapacitation
    IV. Punishment
    V. Educating offenders
   The CORRECT answer is:

   A. I, II   B. I *only*   C. I, II, IV   D. I, III, V
   E. All of the above

2. Populations having *no* influence on criminal sentencing are:
    I. Law students
    II. Police
    III. Social workers
    IV. Magistrates
    V. Parole Officers
   The CORRECT answer is:

   A. I *only*   B. II, IV, V   C. I, II, III   D. I, III, IV
   E. None of the above

3. The *primary* function of a penal code is to provide a means of
    I. *threatening* our enemies
    II. *modifying* behavior patterns
    III. *eliminating* troublemakers
    IV. *protecting* property
    V. *presenting* a moral example of good behavior
   The CORRECT answer is:

   A. I, IV   B. IV *only*   C. II *only*   D. III, IV
   E. All of the above

4. The difference between individual and general crime prevention is that the
    I. *former* can incapacitate individuals
    II. *latter* needs to incapacitate individuals
    III. *latter* emphasizes restraint
    IV. *former* emphasizes deterrence and/or incapacitation
    V. *former* is much more difficult to study
   The CORRECT answer is:

   A. I *only*   B. I, III, V   C. I, III, IV   D. I, II, III, IV
   E. All of the above

5. The view that considers social control to be the *primary* function of the law has the following *disadvantages:* It
    I. is indistinguishable from social engineering
    II. leads to fascism
    III. leads to arbitrary rulings
    IV. leads to dogmatism in jurisprudence
    V. lacks public support
   The CORRECT answer is:

   A. I only   B. II, IV   C. III only   D. I, III, V
   E. I, II, III

6. The evidence shows that criminals *most frequently* consider
    I. their families
    II. costs and benefits
    III. morality
    IV. the law
    V. possible punishment
   The CORRECT answer is:

   A. I only   B. I, IV   C. I, II, V   D. II, III, V   E. II only

7. Norwegian laws against drunk driving tend to prove the criminological theory of
    I. rehabilitationism
    II. retributivism
    III. general prevention
    IV. individual deterrence
    V. lex talones
   The CORRECT answer is:

   A. I, II, V   B. I only   C. III only   D. II, III, IV
   E. All of the above

8. The famous book(s) on jurisprudence written by H.L.A. Hart is(are):
    I. CRIME AND PUNISHMENT
    II. THE LAW AND SOCIETY
    III. PUNISHMENT AND RESPONSIBILITY
    IV. THE CRIME OF PUNISHMENT
    V. LAW, SOCIETY AND PSYCHOTICS
   The CORRECT answer is:

   A. I only   B. II only   C. I, II, V   D. III only   E. III, IV

9. The author of a book advocating rehabilitationism is
    I. H.L.A. Hart
    II. Karl Menninger
    III. Thomas Szasz
    IV. Ivan Illich
    V. Oliver Wendell Holmes
   The CORRECT answer is:

   A. I only   B. II only   C. III only   D. IV only
   E. None of the above

10. THE CRIME OF PUNISHMENT was written by
    I. H.L.A. Hart
    II. Karl Menninger
    III. Thomas Szasz
    IV. Ivan Illich
    V. C. Wright Mills
    The CORRECT answer is:

    A. I only B. II only C. III only D. IV only
    E. None of the above

11. CRIME AND PUNISHMENT was a novel that
    I. was written by Dostoevsky
    II. greatly influenced British jurisprudence
    III. was the first influential book on criminal split-personalities
    IV. popularized crime for existentialists
    V. popularized murder in Russia
    The CORRECT answer is:

    A. I only B. II only C. I, II, V D. I, II, III, IV
    E. I, III, IV

12. A *major* influence on modern rehabilitationist theory in criminology was(were) the philosophical school(s) of:
    I. Positivism
    II. Utilitarianism
    III. Deontology
    IV. Existentialism
    V. Natural Law theory
    The CORRECT answer is:

    A. I only B. II only C. I, II D. III, V
    E. All of the above

13. The point(s) historically included in punishment theory is (are):
    I. The work of the Devil
    II. The work of God
    III. Excusing conditions
    IV. Crimes of passion
    V. Psychiatric counseling
    The CORRECT answer is:

    A. I, IV B. I, II, V C. I, III D. IV only E. III only

14. The thing(s) the law cannot prevent is(are):
    I. Lawbreaking
    II. Lawkeeping
    III. Lawyers
    IV. Judges
    V. Schools
    The CORRECT answer is:

    A. I, III, V B. I only C. III only D. IV, V
    E. All of the above

15. Crimes that CANNOT be prevented include:
    I. Crimes of passion
    II. Civil disobedience
    III. Auto theft
    IV. Drug dealing
    V. Embezzlement
    The CORRECT answer is:

    A. I, II   B. I, II, III   C. I, IV, V   D. IV only
    E. All of the above

16. A person who engages in civil disobedience is one who
    I. is very religious
    II. breaks the law
    III. avoids breaking the law
    IV. acts from passion
    V. acts with premeditation
    The CORRECT answer is:

    A. I, III   B. I, II, III   C. II only   D. III, V
    E. IV, V

17. The thing(s) a civil disobedient must do is(are) to:
    I. Avoid prosecution
    II. Publicize his complaint
    III. Be very conscientious
    IV. Accept legal penalties
    V. Act secretly
    The CORRECT answer is:

    A. I only   B. II, V   C. III only   D. IV only
    E. IV, V

18. The *principal* purpose(s) of entering into civil disobedience is(are) to
    I. prove the sincerity of one's religious beliefs
    II. prove the sincerity of one's political beliefs
    III. change immoral laws
    IV. challenge authoritarian representatives of the law
    V. get publicity
    The CORRECT answer is:

    A. I, IV   B. I, II, III, IV   C. II only   D. III only
    E. III, V

19. The *major* reason(s) that theories of punishment are so important is(are) that:
    I. Being deprived of liberty is harmful
    II. Things that are prima facie wrong need justification
    III. Criminologists need to publish books
    IV. Judges need to refer to academic authorities
    V. Scientific evidence is sufficient to justify punishment
    The CORRECT answer is:

    A. I, II   B. II only   C. I, III, V   D. III, IV, V
    E. None of the above

20. In criminological theories of punishment, MONTERO'S AIM refers to:
    I. A rehabilitationist theory created by Montero
    II. A retributionist theory created by Montero
    III. The theory advocating protecting criminals from the law
    IV. The theory advocating protecting criminals from the
    V. public
    VI. Unpopular laws
    The CORRECT answer is:

    A. II, III   B. I, IV   C. I only   D. V only   E. IV only

21. The *primary* aim(s) of retributionist theories of punishment is(are) to:
    I. Insure that criminals atone for their wrongs
    II. Encourage would-be criminals to abstain from crime
    III. Deter crime
    IV. Enforce the law
    V. Reform offenders
    The CORRECT answer is:

    A. I only   B. I, II, IV   C. II, III   D. IV, V   E. I, IV

22. The theory called *"retribution in distribution"* advocates that criminals should suffer
    I. in proportion to their crime
    II. to encourage others to desist
    III. but not at all costs
    IV. for their crimes at all costs
    V. penalties identical to those of their victims
    The CORRECT answer is:

    A. I, V   B. II only   C. I, II   D. III only   E. IV only

23. According to *"brute retributivism,"* punishment is
    I. little more than a thirst for revenge
    II. socially satisfying
    III. a crowd pleaser
    IV. a general deterrence
    V. a reforming agent
    The CORRECT answer is:

    A. I only   B. I, II, V   C. I, II, III   D. II, III, IV
    E. III, IV, V

24. The concept(s) *very important* to punishment theory is(are):
    I. Intentions
    II. Passions
    III. Statistics
    IV. Logic
    V. Operant conditioning
    The CORRECT answer is:

    A. I, II   B. I only   C. III only   D. III, IV   E. I, II, V

25. Both rehabilitationists and retributionists can agree that the *outstanding* flaw(s) in the criminal justice system is(are):
    I. Procedural injustice
    II. Influence of criminologists
    III. Patriarchal influences
    IV. Medical intervention
    V. Appeals to higher courts
    The CORRECT answer is:

    A. I only   B. II, III   C. I, III   D. IV only   E. I, II, III

26. Achieving social justice through the criminal law must be balanced against
    I. an oppressive criminal justice system
    II. overly stringent laws
    III. principles of liberty
    IV. due process
    V. rights of privacy
    The CORRECT answer is:

    A. I only   B. I, II, V   C. I, III, IV   D. I, II, III, IV
    E. All of the above

27. The *important* concept(s) that *must* underlie fair judicial decisions include(s):
    I. Precedence
    II. Consistency
    III. Impartiality
    IV. Discretion
    V. Leniency
    The CORRECT answer is:

    A. I only   B. II only   C. I, II, V   D. I, II, III
    E. I, II, IV, V

28. If there is a spurt in crime in a given area, and more police are located there, after which crime rates return to normal, it is *reasonable* to conclude that
    I. the police apprehended the criminals
    II. the police found the cause of the crime
    III. the police presence caused the drop in crime
    IV. the community should increase its police force
    V. detectives participated in the crime resolution
    The CORRECT answer is:

    A. I only   B. I, II   C. I, III   D. III only   E. I, IV

29. Convicted murderers with high recidivism rates *usually* get arrested for
    I. murder
    II. assault
    III. aggravated assault
    IV. auto theft
    V. grand larceny
    The CORRECT answer is:

    A. I only   B. I, II   C. II only   D. III, IV   E. III only

30. A California study of comparative recidivism rates between retributivism and rehabilitationism concluded that
    I. rehabilitation had lower recidivism rates
    II. retributionism had lower recidivism rates
    III. neither recidivism rate was lower than the other
    IV. the study was inconclusive
    V. more rehabilitation programs should be created
    The CORRECT answer is:

    A. I only   B. II only   C. III only   D. IV only
    E. None of the above

31. The factor(s) that appear(s) to increase recidivism is(are):
    I. Keeping people in prison longer
    II. Keeping people in prison more briefly
    III. Refusing to imprison people
    IV. Peer pressure
    V. Temptations to commit crime
    The CORRECT answer is:

    A. I only   B. II only   C. II, III   D. II, IV   E. IV only

32. The improvement(s) that rehabilitation programs achieve over retributivist programs is(are):
    I. They cost less
    II. A higher suicide rate among prisoners
    III. A lower suicide rate among prisoners
    IV. Better relations between inmates and prison staff
    V. They require fewer professionals to implement
    The CORRECT answer is:

    A. I only   B. II, IV   C. III only   D. I, III   E. IV only

33. Dr. Thomas Szasz's MAIN criticism(s) against rehabilitation approaches to punishment is(are) that they
    I. don't work
    II. cost more
    III. treat bad people as sick
    IV. treat sick people as bad
    V. don't use enough professions
    The CORRECT answer is:

    A. I, II   B. IV only   C. III only   D. IV only
    E. II, IV

34. Evidence to date does NOT support the claim(s) that
    I. deterrence is a worthy goal
    II. deterrence is increasing
    III. convicted persons are mentally ill
    IV. convicted persons are sane
    V. prison facilities are inadequate
    The CORRECT answer is:

    A. I, III   B. I, IV   C. II only   D. III only   E. IV only

35. The motive(s) frequently discounted for criminal behavior is(are)
    I. revenge
    II. retaliation
    III. profit
    IV. hostility
    V. necessity
    The CORRECT answer is:

    A. I only   B. II only   C. III,V   D. IV only   E. I, IV

36. A reductivist approach to sentencing recommends that we
    I. increase minimum sentences
    II. decrease lengths of minimum sentences
    III. increase maximum sentences
    IV. decrease maximum sentences
    V. eliminate plea bargaining
    The CORRECT answer is:

    A. I, II   B. II only   C. III only   D. II, IV
    E. None of the above

37. Lengthy sentences are usually the result of
    I. hanging judges
    II. inept lawyers
    III. an increase in serious offenses
    IV. indeterminate sentences
    V. administrative error
    The CORRECT answer is:

    A. I, III   B. II only   C. II, IV   D. IV only.
    E. All of the above

38. The general deterrence approach to punishment and crime prevention works *least well* with respect to
    I. crimes of passion
    II. premeditated crimes
    III. professional criminals
    IV. occasional criminals
    V. white collar crimes
    The CORRECT answer is:

    A. I only   B. II, IV   C. II, III   D. III only
    E. None of the above

39. Methodological difficulties involved in criminological research include :
    I. Determining criteria for success and failure
    II. Adequately classifying population groups
    III. Getting adequate sample populations
    IV. Properly interpreting motivation
    V. Mathematical computations
    The CORRECT answer is:

    A. I, II   B. II, III   C. I, II, III   D. IV only
    E. All of the above

40. In evaluating the long-term effects of punishment upon criminals, one should take into account
    I.   constructive uses of leisure
    II. educational enhancement
    III. neighbors' opinions
    IV. attitudinal changes
    V.   public reaction to ex-convicts

    The CORRECT answer is:

    A. I, II   B. III *only*   C. I, II, III   D. I, II, IV
    E. All of the above

41. The significant distinction(s) to make in studies of long-term effects of punishment is(are) *between*
    I.   violent and non-violent crimes
    II. offenders who get caught and the ones who do not
    III. occasional vs. habitual recidivists
    IV. Men and women offenders
    V.   Youthful vs. adult offenders

    The CORRECT answer is:

    A. I *only*   B. II *only*   C. I, III   D. III *only*
    E. I, II, IV

42. The disadvantage(s) of being treated for mental illness as opposed to being punished for criminal behavior is(are) that
    I.   a diagnosis of the illness is difficult to find
    II. cures are very rare
    III. mental patients don't have the stringent legal protections prisoners have
    IV. it is harder to pick up crime tips
    V.   medical personnel agree on prognoses

    The CORRECT answer is:

    A. I, II   B. I *only*   C. III *only*   D. I, II, IV
    E. I, III

43. The assumption(s) from the field of psychology that has (have) led some criminologists to become rehabilitationists is(are):
    I.   Humans act rationally
    II. Human behavior is the result of antecedent causes
    III. Basic fears motivate humans
    IV. The pleasure principle motivates everyone
    V.   Humans act irrationally

    The CORRECT answer is:

    A. I *only*   B. II, V   C. III *only*   D. IV *only*
    E. All of the above

44. Historically, the transition from retributionism to re-habilitationism in crime prevention and treatment corresponds to the
    I. transition from natural law theory to science
    II. rise of capitalism
    III. growth of professional criminals
    IV. changes in public attitudes toward crime
    V. establishment of law in colonial America
    The CORRECT answer is:

    A. I only   B. II only   C. I, II   D. II, III   E. IV only

45. Various roles undertaken by police officers include:
    I. Information gathering
    II. Maintaining order
    III. Enforcing the law
    IV. Serving the public
    V. Counseling victims
    The CORRECT answer is:

    A. I, II   B. II, III, IV, V   C. II, III   D. III, IV
    E. All of the above

46. When police officers maintain order, they usually are
    I. issuing a summons
    II. making an arrest
    III. resolving a dispute
    IV. gathering data for the courts
    V. counseling victims
    The CORRECT answer is:

    A. I only   B. II only   C. I, III   D. III only
    E. All of the above

47. The *majority* of arrests made by police originate from
    I. citizens' complaints
    II. police observation of street incidents
    III. anonymous tip-offs
    IV. underworld informers
    V. computerized records
    The CORRECT answer is:

    A. I only   B. II only   C. II, III   D. I, III, IV
    E. IV only

48. Detectives' contributions to arrest rates can *best* be characterized as:
    I. They make up the largest portion of them
    II. They contribute to approximately 15-20% of them
    III. They barely contribute to arrests at all
    IV. Ancillary
    V. Obstructive
    The CORRECT answer is:

    A. I only   B. II only   C. III only   D. IV only
    E. None of the above

49. The *most important* group(s) influencing police effectiveness is(are):   49.____
    I. criminals
    II. courts
    III. judges
    IV. citizens
    V. social workers
    The CORRECT answer is:

    A. I *only*   B. II, III   C. III, IV, V   D. IV *only*
    E. All of the above

50. The significant factor(s) in long-term studies of criminal behavior and the effectiveness of   50.____
    punishment is(are):
    I. Whether the criminal's marriage survived
    II. The parole officer's reports
    III. The psychiatric social worker
    IV. Alcoholism
    V. Educational achievement
    The CORRECT answer is:

    A. I *only*   B. I, II   C. II *only*   D. I, II, III
    E. All of the above

KEY (CORRECT ANSWERS)

1. E	11. E	21. E	31. A	41. C
2. E	12. B	22. D	32. E	42. C
3. C	13. E	23. C	33. D	43. B
4. C	14. B	24. B	34. D	44. A
5. A	15. A	25. A	35. C	45. E
6. E	16. D	26. E	36. E	46. D
7. C	17. D	27. D	37. D	47. A
8. D	18. D	28. D	38. A	48. B
9. B	19. A	29. E	39. E	49. D
10. B	20. E	30. C	40. D	50. B

EXAMINATION SECTION
TEST 1

DIRECTIONS: Each question or incomplete statement is followed by several suggested answers or completions. Select the one that BEST answers the question or completes the statement. *PRINT THE LETTER OF THE CORRECT ANSWER IN THE SPACE AT THE RIGHT.*

1. In which of the following situations would local police NOT be justified in conducting a search without a search warrant?

    A. Seizure of nonphysical evidence, such as an overheard conversation
    B. An automobile is searched because it is believed to have been involved in a crime
    C. A search of a person is made incident to a lawful arrest
    D. A search of a private residence if a suspected criminal is seen fleeing into the residence

1.____

2. Which of the following is NOT generally viewed as a purpose of community-based corrections?
    To

    A. protect first-time or nonserious offenders from the stigma and pain of imprisonment
    B. reduce the expense of supervising inmates
    C. increase the scrutiny to which an inmate's rehabilitation process is subjected
    D. protect the prisons system from an overwhelming influx of prisoners

2.____

3. Under a typical prison administrative structure, the function of keeping inmate records is usually performed by the department led by the

    A. associate warden for classification and treatment
    B. associate warden for custody
    C. business manager
    D. medical services manager

3.____

4. Under prescribed conditions, and for certain types of offenses, law enforcement officers may issue citations in lieu of arrest. A citation in lieu of arrest is warranted in each of the following situations EXCEPT

    A. the accused is identified as a member of the local community
    B. it is not yet determinable where the accused will appear to answer charges
    C. the offense is a misdemeanor where there is no danger of physical harm
    D. there is no reason to believe that the accused will flee from the jurisdiction

4.____

5. Although there is no set standard for how *speedy* a criminal defendant's trial must be, the Federal Speedy Trial Act of 1970 mandates _____ days from arrest to indictment, and _____ days from indictment to trial.

    A. 10; 30   B. 15; 45   C. 30; 70   D. 60; 120

5.____

6. In the nineteenth century, some prisons used the _____ system, in which officials sold the labor of inmates to private businesses.

    A. convict-lease   B. state account
    C. contract   D. Auburn

6.____

7. Acts that are outlawed because they violate basic moral values, such as rape, murder, assault, and robbery, are known as _____ crimes.

   A. mala in se
   B. hate
   C. mala prohibitum
   D. instrumental

8. Which of the following statements is NOT an accurate description of the general demographics of crime in the United States?

   A. The effect of income has little influence on black crime rates.
   B. Poor whites are more violent than affluent whites.
   C. Most crimes are committed by people aged 18-25.
   D. Lower-class juvenile girls are more criminal than upper-class girls.

9. When a jail term is made a condition of probation, the court has implemented a form of correction known as

   A. split sentencing
   B. shock probation
   C. intensive probation
   D. shock incarceration

10. United States court rulings have provided each of the following as a federally mandated guideline for local police in their application of the Miranda rule EXCEPT

    A. people who are mentally ill due to clinically diagnosed schizophrenia may voluntarily confess and waive their Miranda rights
    B. suspects must be aware of all the possible outcomes of waiving their rights in order for the Miranda warning to be considered properly given
    C. evidence that is obtained in violation of the Miranda rule may be used by the government to impeach a defendant's testimony during trial
    D. the erroneous admission of a coerced confession at trial can be ruled a *harmless error* that would not automatically result in overturning a conviction

11. In the criminal justice system, what is the term for the set of facts and circumstances that would induce a reasonably intelligent and prudent person to believe that an accused person had committed a specific crime?

    A. Reasonable doubt
    B. Probable cause
    C. Warranted suspicion
    D. Burden of proof

12. In the court case Procunier v. Martinez, it was ruled that

    A. a prison inmate had the right to have adequate medical care
    B. an inmate's mail could be censored only if there existed substantial belief that its contents would threaten security
    C. the right of an inmate to grant press interviews could be limited
    D. the practice of double-bunking inmates in a small cell was not unconstitutional

13. Which of the following statements about murder in the United States is FALSE?

    A. Most victims know or are acquainted with their assailant.
    B. Most murders involve firearms.
    C. Most murders occur during the commission of a felony.
    D. Murder rates are highest in the South and West.

14. In most United States communities, the primary function of the local police can best be described as

    A. peace-keeping, dispute-settling agents of public health and safety
    B. symbols of public morality and stability
    C. investigators of crime and enforcers of the rule of law
    D. providers of emergency services

15. Most prison inmates in the United States are serving time for

    A. drug trafficking   B. burglary
    C. robbery   D. larceny

16. In general, the personality of members of the law enforcement community is characterized by each of the following EXCEPT

    A. insecurity   B. individualism
    C. conservatism   D. secrecy

17. Reducing burglaries in a housing project by increasing lighting and installing security alarms is an example of

    A. absolute deterrence   B. diffusion of benefits
    C. discouragement   D. situational crime prevention

18. Each of the following is considered to be a pre-trial process EXCEPT

    A. booking   B. detention
    C. arraignment   D. grand jury examination

19. The Differential _____ Theory explains criminal behavior by postulating that when people consider the available legitimate and illegitimate behaviors, they select the alternative that is perceived to be the best.

    A. Identification   B. Association Reinforcement
    C. Anticipation   D. Association

20. Any *offensive touching* is known in criminal terms as

    A. abuse   B. battery   C. rape   D. assault

21. The modern American police department was born out of urban mob violence that occurred in the United States during the _____ century.

    A. late seventeenth   B. late eighteenth
    C. early nineteenth   D. early twentieth

22. Each of the following is a system that has been developed in the American criminal justice system for providing legal counsel to the indigent EXCEPT

    A. assigning private attorneys on a case-by-case basis
    B. creating a publicly funded defender's office
    C. assigning attorneys from other courts—juvenile, probate, or district courts—on a rotating basis
    D. contracting with a law firm or group of private attorneys to regularly provide services

23. What is the term for the revocation of a person's probationary status for violation of probation rules? 23.____

    A. Alternative sanction
    B. Technical violation
    C. Status offense
    D. Determinate sentencing

24. According to most surveys and research, approximately what percentage of their working hours do most local police devote to crime-related activity? 24.____

    A. 1-5   B. 10-25   C. 40-60   D. 55-75

25. Which of the following choice theories of crime best shows the relationship between crime and punishment? 25.____

    A. Specific deterrence
    B. Rational choice
    C. Incapacitation
    D. General deterrence

KEY (CORRECT ANSWERS)

1. D		11. B	
2. C		12. B	
3. A		13. C	
4. B		14. A	
5. C		15. C	
6. C		16. B	
7. A		17. D	
8. D		18. C	
9. A		19. C	
10. B		20. B	

21. C
22. C
23. B
24. B
25. D

TEST 2

DIRECTIONS: Each question or incomplete statement is followed by several suggested answers or completions. Select the one that BEST answers the question or completes the statement. *PRINT THE LETTER OF THE CORRECT ANSWER IN THE SPACE AT THE RIGHT.*

1. Approximately what percentage of the United States correctional population is on probation?

    A. 10   B. 30   C. 65   D. 80

    1.____

2. A criminal case that is tried afresh, as if there had been no earlier decision in a lower court, is said to be tried

    A. cum laude
    B. a priori
    C. de novo
    D. pro bono

    2.____

3. Which of the following is a crime-specific policing strategy?

    A. Problem-oriented policing
    B. Crackdown
    C. Team policing
    D. Aggressive preventive patrol

    3.____

4. In their work on personality and crime, Glueck and Glueck identified a number of personality traits that they believed characterized antisocial youth. Which of the following is NOT one of these?

    A. Narcissism
    B. Introversion
    C. Sadism
    D. Impulsiveness

    4.____

5. Early problems with the first local police departments in the United States were most clearly due to

    A. lack of formal training
    B. unclear statutes concerning private property
    C. an abundance of non-police functions
    D. supervision by elected political officials

    5.____

6. The earliest treatment programs used in United States prisons tended to be

    A. structured psychological treatments
    B. vocational
    C. educational
    D. informal counseling

    6.____

7. Which of the following statements is in line with a criminal defendant's right to be free from *double jeopardy*?

    I. If a defendant is tried and convicted of murder in New York, he cannot be tried again for the same murder in New York.
    II. If a defendant is tried in federal court for a crime, he cannot be tried in state court for the same crime.
    III. If a single act violates the laws of two states, the offender may only be punished by one of the states.

    The CORRECT answer is:

    A. I only   B. II only   C. I, III   D. II, III

    7.____

77

8. A state of normlessness in society, which may be caused by decreased homogeneity and which provides a setting conducive to crimes and other antisocial acts, is known as

   A. anomie B. discord C. inequity D. ennui

9. Which of the following events would occur earliest in the cycle of *secondary deviance* as proposed by Edwin Lemert?

   A. Offense escalation
   B. Assumption of deviant identity
   C. Deviant self-labeling
   D. Legal reprisals

10. The first privately-run state prison in the United States was opened in Marion, Kentucky in

    A. 1941 B. 1968 C. 1975 D. 1986

11. A _____, granted by the president or state governor, is an exercise of the extraordinary power to change a criminal punishment to one less severe.

    A. commutation of sentence B. reprieve
    C. pardon D. set-aside judgment

12. Which of the following is a document filed in juvenile court alleging that a juvenile is a delinquent, a status offender, or a dependent, and asking that the juvenile be transferred to a criminal court for prosecution as an adult?

    A. Charge document B. Petition
    C. Indictment D. Disposition

13. Approximately what percentage of United States prison inmates have had a history of substance abuse?

    A. 20 B. 40 C. 60 D. 80

14. Which of the following are rulings made by the Supreme Court concerning a criminal defendant's right to a trial by a jury?
    I. When a 12-person jury is used, the Sixth Amendment does not require a unanimous verdict, except in first-degree murder cases.
    II. A 6-person jury will fulfill a defendant's right to trial by jury.
    III. In all capital cases, a 12-person jury must be used and the verdict must be unanimous.

    The CORRECT answer is:

    A. I only B. III only C. I, II D. II, III

15. The branch of social science that uses the scientific method of the natural sciences, and which suggests that human behavior is a product of social, biological, psychological, or economic forces, is called

    A. animism B. positivism
    C. syncretism D. behaviorism

16. In prisons, the most traditional type of inmate treatment involves 16._____

    A. vocational rehabilitation
    B. educational programs
    C. private industry
    D. psychological counseling and therapy

17. Approximately what percentage of robberies in the United States are stranger-to- 17._____
    stranger crimes?

    A. 10   B. 30   C. 50   D. 75

18. Which of the following is NOT generally considered to be a weakness associated with 18._____
    United States juvenile courts today?

    A. A generalized lack of resources
    B. Problems created by the diversity of the courts' roles
    C. A reputation for dealing too harshly with young offenders
    D. The inferior position most juvenile courts hold in the court hierarchy

19. The process perspective of crime focuses on the _____ forces involved in influencing 19._____
    criminal behavior.

    A. situational   B. socialization
    C. economic/political   D. ecological

20. The right to _____ has undergone the most modification in the relatively recent prolifer- 20._____
    ation of child-abuse cases in United States courts.

    A. be free from double jeopardy
    B. confront witnesses
    C. legal counsel
    D. a speedy and public trial

21. In general, the _____ is considered to be the core element of the American criminal jus- 21._____
    tice system.

    A. criminal court   B. sheriff's department
    C. Supreme Court   D. corrections system

22. In recent years, _____ crimes have overtaken other forms of crime in terms of the num- 22._____
    ber of court commitments in the United States.

    A. violent   B. public-order
    C. property   D. drug

23. A person in the United States who is convicted of a felony offense loses all civil rights. 23._____
    The term for this loss is

    A. attainder   B. divestiture
    C. disenfranchisement   D. rejoinder

24. The Safe Streets and Crime Control Act of _____ provided for the expenditure of fed- 24._____
    eral funds for state and local crime control efforts.

    A. 1948   B. 1968   C. 1981   D. 1988

25. Which of the following was a United States penal reformer who introduced the idea of releasing prisoners once they had been reformed? 25._____

    A. August Vollmer   B. Robert Peel
    C. Zebulon Brockway   D. Walter Crofton

KEY (CORRECT ANSWERS)

1. C 11. A
2. C 12. B
3. B 13. D
4. B 14. C
5. D 15. B

6. C 16. D
7. A 17. D
8. A 18. C
9. C 19. B
10. D 20. B

21. A
22. D
23. A
24. B
25. C

EXAMINATION SECTION
TEST 1

DIRECTIONS: Each question or incomplete statement is followed by several suggested answers or completions. Select the one that BEST answers the question or completes the statement. *PRINT THE LETTER OF THE CORRECT ANSWER IN THE SPACE AT THE RIGHT.*

1. Most research that has been conducted on the issue of rehabilitating criminals in the United States has revealed that

    A. rehabilitation efforts are more likely to work if an offender receives individual attention from the system
    B. in general, rehabilitation efforts have no appreciable effect on recidivism
    C. rehabilitation through the medical model has proven to be slightly more effective than vocational or educational programs
    D. offenders who go through some type of rehabilitation program are not nearly as likely to recidivate as offenders who are merely incarcerated

2. Unlawfully obtaining, or attempting to obtain the property of another by the threat of eventual injury or harm to that person, the person's property, or another person is an offense classified officially as

    A. extortion   B. aggravated assault
    C. terrorism   D. blackmail

3. The current explanation for female crime in the United States focuses on

    A. the *chivalry hypothesis* of hidden female crime
    B. the social role of women in society
    C. the *masculinity hypothesis* of females who commit crime
    D. economic status

4. Which of the following crimes generally has no statute of limitations?

    A. Robbery   B. Murder
    C. Rape   D. Embezzlement

5. In general, proponents of the due process model of criminal justice tend to be

    A. representatives of the business lobby
    B. members of the legal profession who see themselves as protectors of civil rights
    C. members of the legal profession who vigorously prosecute criminal offenses
    D. victims of violent crime

6. Which of the following principles is NOT included in a noninterventional justice philosophy?

    A. Decarceration   B. Rehabilitation
    C. Diversion   D. Decriminalization

7. Which of the following views of crime asserts that offenses can be expected if there is a suitable target that is not protected by capable guardians?
The

    A. rational choice view   B. medical model
    C. developmental view   D. routine activities view

8. The charge of second-degree murder requires the actor to have

   A. premeditation
   B. dissent
   C. deliberation
   D. malice aforethought

9. In the United States correctional system, probationary sentences are granted by each of the following EXCEPT _____ courts.

   A. state superior
   B. state district
   C. municipal
   D. federal district

10. Each of the following factors has been shown to have a direct correlation to the incidence of spouse abuse EXCEPT

    A. education level
    B. the presence of alcohol
    C. military service
    D. economic stress

11. Which of the following occurs at the latest stage in the criminal justice process?

    A. Bail considered
    B. Arraignment
    C. Plea negotiations
    D. Custody

12. Some critics of the American criminal justice system argue that it is a political entity that operates subjectively, with some cases receiving the full attention of the law, while others are settled with a minimum of due process. This idea is known as the _____ model of justice.

    A. caste
    B. wedding cake
    C. medical
    D. Marxist

13. Which of the following is characteristic of a *watchman* style of policing?

    A. Formal authority both within the department and between officers and the public
    B. An emphasis on community relations
    C. Low turnover
    D. Relatively infrequent arrests

14. Which of the following is/are considered to be serious limitations or drawbacks associated with the use of self-report studies for measuring crime?
    I. Their accuracy in determining the behavior of chronic offenders
    II. Their accuracy in determining the behavior of persistent drug abusers
    III. Their validity and reliability in measuring youth crimes

    The CORRECT answer is:

    A. I only
    B. II only
    C. I, II
    D. II, III

15. Each of the following is considered a factor that would render a punishment of a criminal *cruel and unusual* and therefore unconstitutional EXCEPT

    A. it shocks the general conscience and is fundamentally unfair
    B. the punishment degrades the dignity of human beings
    C. it involves physical discomfort or mental uncertainty
    D. it is more severe than the offense for which it has been given

16. Which of the following is NOT typically a responsibility assigned to a correctional officer? 16.____

    A. Protecting inmates from other inmates
    B. Preventing escapes
    C. Making sure inmates are adequately fed
    D. Controlling inmate movement within the institution

17. In a typical state judicial system, the highest court with general jurisdiction may be called by any of the names below EXCEPT 17.____

    A. superior court
    B. court of common pleas
    C. intermediate appellate court
    D. circuit court

18. What is the term for a written order issued by a judicial officer that requires a person accused of a criminal offense to appear in a designated court at a specified time to answer the charges? 18.____

    A. Indictment   B. Summons
    C. Injunction   D. Subpoena

19. The _____ theory of crime states that material goals pervade all aspects of American life, and therefore crime rates are high in American culture. 19.____

    A. institutional anomie   B. focal concern
    C. behavioral   D. relative deprivation

20. The logical argument behind the concept of _____ is that as long as criminals are in prison, they cannot be on the streets committing crimes. 20.____

    A. conditional release   B. incapacitation
    C. restitution   D. deterrence

21. What is the term for the legal principle by which the decision or holding in an earlier case becomes the standard by which subsequent similar cases are judged? 21.____

    A. Presentment   B. Caveat emptor
    C. Summation   D. Stare decisis

22. As an alternative to bail in some courts, a criminal defendant is released with no immediate requirement of payment. However, if the defendant fails to appear, he or she is liable for the full amount.
    This system is known as 22.____

    A. deposit bail   B. surety bail
    C. unsecured bail   D. conditional release

23. A common pathway to crime begins at an early age with stubborn behavior and defiance of parents. These behaviors lead to defiance and disobedience, and then to authority avoidances such as truancy or running away.
    This is known as the _____ pathway. 23.____

    A. classical   B. overt
    C. covert   D. authority conflict

24. According to most research, the rearrest rate for prison inmates who are paroled in the United States is about _____ percent.

    A. 30 B. 45 C. 60 D. 90

25. The exclusionary rule in criminal justice proceedings is based upon the rights granted in the _____ Amendment to the Constitution.

    A. First B. Second C. Fourth D. Fifth

KEY (CORRECT ANSWERS)

1. B
2. A
3. D
4. B
5. B

6. B
7. D
8. D
9. C
10. A

11. C
12. B
13. D
14. C
15. C

16. C
17. C
18. B
19. A
20. B

21. D
22. C
23. D
24. C
25. C

TEST 2

DIRECTIONS: Each question or incomplete statement is followed by several suggested answers or completions. Select the one that BEST answers the question or completes the statement. *PRINT THE LETTER OF THE CORRECT ANSWER IN THE SPACE AT THE RIGHT.*

1. The recidivism rate of probationers in the United States is _____ than the recidivism rate of prison inmates.

    A. much higher
    B. somewhat higher
    C. somewhat lower
    D. much lower

2. To prove that a murder has taken place, most state jurisdictions require prosecutors to prove that the accused

    A. was provoked into a crime of passion
    B. intentionally and with malice desired the death of the victim
    C. understood at the time of the murder that killing was wrong
    D. was of sound mind when the crime occurred

3. What is the term for the process in which a potential jury panel is questioned by the prosecution and defense to select jurors who are unbiased and objective?

    A. Nolle prosequi
    B. Voir dire
    C. Venire
    D. Peremptory challenge

4. Approximately how many law enforcement agencies are administered by the United States government?

    A. 6   B. 18   C. 35   D. 50

5. The idea that criminal acts are related to a person's exposure to an excess amount of antisocial attitudes and values is known as the principle of

    A. differential association
    B. interactionism
    C. deinstitutionalization
    D. degenerate anomalies

6. Which of the following would NOT typically be classified as a status offense?

    A. Shoplifting
    B. Curfew violation
    C. Possession of alcohol
    D. Truancy

7. In which of the following court cases was it ruled that the death penalty may be applied when aggravating circumstances exist in a murder case, such as murder for profit?

    A. Powell v. Alabama (1932)
    B. Benton v. Maryland (1969)
    C. Gregg v. Georgia (1981)
    D. Rhodes v. Chapman (1981)

8. Which of the following was a utilitarian philosopher whose works helped spawn the classical theory of criminal behavior?

    A. Karl Marx
    B. Cesare Beccaria
    C. Emile Durkheim
    D. Enrico Ferri

9. State sentencing codes usually include various factors that can legitimately influence the length of prison sentences. Which of the following is NOT one of these factors?

    A. The offender's prior criminal record
    B. Whether the offender used weapons
    C. Whether the crime was committed for money
    D. The offender's economic status

10. Research on the prison culture in today's correctional institutions has revealed each of the following EXCEPT

    A. newer inmates tend to be younger than before and disdainful of older inmates
    B. white inmates are much more cohesively organized than black or Latin inmates
    C. more inmates than ever are assigned to protective custody
    D. those who adapt best to the prison culture are the least likely to reform on the outside

11. In the crime of larceny, a victim willingly gives up temporary possession of property, but retains legal ownership. This is known as

    A. constructive intent
    B. custodial convenience
    C. noncoercive larceny
    D. constructive possession

12. In most local police departments, the majority of officers are assigned to

    A. identifying public-order crimes
    B. traffic control
    C. patrol work
    D. investigations

13. Which of the following offers the best example to a *good faith exception* to the exclusionary rule?

    A. The police use of overflights to spy on marijuana growers without the use of a warrant
    B. The unauthorized taping, by a civilian, of a telephone conversation involving a second party who is unaware that the conversation is being recorded
    C. The coercion of a confession from a violent killer who is a flight risk
    D. A stop-and-frisk of persons outside a building that is known to house a drug operation, without the use of a warrant

14. People who favor the death penalty in America, and yet criticize its failure to act as a real deterrent, usually focus their criticism on the _____ of the punishment.

    A. severity
    B. certainty
    C. privacy
    D. swiftness

15. A criminal court whose trial jurisdiction includes no felonies, and which may or may not hear appeals, is known as a court of _____ jurisdiction.

    A. limited
    B. appellate
    C. criminal
    D. general

16. Which of the following statements about local police investigations is true? 16.____

    A. Suspects are usually identified before a detective is assigned to a case.
    B. The majority of solved cases involved the gathering of data and evidence by detectives away from the crime scene.
    C. Detectives spend an average of 2-5 days on each case.
    D. A mastery of investigative techniques is usually the most significant element involved in solving crimes.

17. The primary goal of intensive probation supervision as a means of correction is 17.____

    A. reintegration   B. punishment
    C. diversion   D. control

18. What is the term for a government agency or subunit that receives and screens juvenile referrals from police, or from other agencies or persons? 18.____

    A. Booking room   B. Intake unit
    C. Disposition unit   D. Diagnosis center

19. Which of the following types of treatment, administered to prison inmates, uses tokens to reward conformity and develop positive behavior traits? 19.____

    A. Reality therapy   B. Behavior therapy
    C. Transactional analysis   D. Social therapy

20. Forcible rape is coerced 20.____
    I. sexual intercourse induced by the threat of social, economic, or vocational harm
    II. participation of a male in intercourse or other sexual activity by a female
    III. sexual intercourse induced by the threat of physical harm
    IV. participation in oral sex
    The CORRECT answer is:

    A. I only   B. I, II, III   C. III only   D. III, IV

21. Within the criminal justice system, the _____ typically represent the first step in deterring crime. 21.____

    A. police   B. prosecution
    C. communities   D. correctional officers

22. Which of the following individuals has been credited with pioneering the concept of probation? 22.____

    A. August Vollmer   B. Cesare Beccaria
    C. Karl Marx   D. John Augustus

23. In the majority of states, state court judges are selected 23.____

    A. by an executive council elected by the state assembly
    B. through popular election
    C. by the state senate
    D. by means of gubernatorial appointment

24. Which of the following factors is LEAST likely to be correlated with the crime of child abuse?   24.____

    A. Family isolation
    B. Parents with little or no secondary or higher-level education
    C. Familial stress
    D. Parents who have suffered abuse

25. The criticism currently leveled against the practice of parole in the United States includes each of the following arguments EXCEPT   25.____

    A. the process has the unintended effect of granting an inmate too much power and control over the path his or her future may take
    B. it is beyond the capacity of parole authorities to predict who will make a successful judgment on parole, or to accurately monitor their behavior in the community
    C. the procedures that control the decision to grant parole are vague and have not been controlled by due process considerations
    D. it is unjust to decide whether to release an individual from prison based on what we expect that person to do in the future

---

KEY (CORRECT ANSWERS)

1. C		11. D	
2. B		12. C	
3. B		13. A	
4. D		14. B	
5. A		15. A	
6. A		16. A	
7. C		17. C	
8. B		18. B	
9. D		19. B	
10. B		20. C	

21. A
22. D
23. B
24. B
25. A

EXAMINATION SECTION
TEST 1

DIRECTIONS: Each question or incomplete statement is followed by several suggested answers or completions. Select the one that BEST answers the question or completes the statement. *PRINT THE LETTER OF THE CORRECT ANSWER IN THE SPACE AT THE RIGHT.*

1. Studies of the distribution of crime in cities have produced remarkably consistent results showing that burglaries, robberies, and serious assaults occur in areas with certain characteristics.
   Which one of the following is LEAST likely to be a characteristic of a high crime rate area?
   A

   A. mixed land use
   B. high population density
   C. low rate of home ownership
   D. low proportion of single males
   E. high proportion of working mothers

2. Most modern police administrators recommend the licensing of private police officers. Which one of the following is LEAST appropriate as a required provision for the licensing of private officers?
   All

   A. private patrolmen should be required to post a surety bond
   B. private patrolmen should be required to have their license renewed annually
   C. private patrolmen should be allowed to carry a weapon, in accordance with state and local law
   D. licensed private patrolmen and private patrol organizations should be required to furnish an up-to-date list of clients periodically
   E. private patrolmen should be required to wear a uniform similar in design and color to that of the municipal police

3. A police commander has an important role in the control of prostitution. Which one of the following observations concerning prostitution is LEAST likely to be accurate?

   A. Prostitution has been commercialized by organized crime.
   B. Direct contact with prostitutes is the most important source of venereal disease.
   C. Prostitution serves as an outlet for the sale of narcotics.
   D. Male homosexual prostitution is more difficult to control than female prostitution.
   E. The patrons of both male homosexual prostitutes and female prostitutes are often the victims of blackmail and extortion.

4. The President's Commission on Law Enforcement and Administration of Justice made a thorough study of organized crime.
   Which one of the following is LEAST likely to be an observation made by the Commission as to the structure of an organized crime *family*?

A. Each *family* has a second-in-command who is the only person with authority to act in the absence of the *boss*.
B. There is one all-powerful *boss* at the head of each crime *family* whose authority in all matters relating to his *family* is absolute.
C. Many *families* have a clearly defined staff person who assumes responsibility for intimate counsel to the *boss*, but has no authority.
D. There is maintained in each *family* a position of *enforcer* whose duty is to arrange for the maiming and killing of erring *family* members.
E. The *soldiers* are the people who do most of the actual work (take bets, answer telephones, sell narcotics) in the various *family* enterprises.

5. The concept of staff inspection is widely discussed in police literature and is of extreme importance to a police commander, especially in a large police organization.
Which one of the following statements concerning the creation and functioning of a staff inspection unit is LEAST likely to be accurate?

A. Its creation and functioning removes inspectional responsibility from line personnel.
B. Such a unit, by definition, must be established outside the normal lines of authority.
C. The need for the creation of a staff inspection unit becomes more pronounced as a department becomes more decentralized.
D. Such a unit can legitimately concern itself with determining whether or not manpower is distributed in accordance with an analysis of need.
E. Such a unit can properly concern itself with whether or not command personnel are operating within the framework of announced department policy.

6. Police must become more concerned with the processes by which people interact with each other and perceive each other.
Which one of the following basic terms, used in describing the relationship of people with each other, is LEAST properly defined?

A. Prejudice - a judgment about a thing or group, based upon comparisons and examinations of fact
B. Projection - the act of attributing one's own personal shortcomings and faults to other people
C. Hatred - a long-lasting, deep-rooted emotion, more often felt toward whole classes of people as opposed to individuals
D. Anger - a transitory emotional state, usually directed at individuals, which is often followed by feelings of repentance
E. Rationalization - the act of attempting to find acceptable *reasons* to justify behavior and attitudes whose true reasons for existence are unacceptable

7. The President's Commission on Law Enforcement and Administration of Justice obtained data from various sources on the victims of crime. This data shows some very interesting relationships which may very well have nationwide application.
Based on this data, which one of the following statements concerning the victims of violent crimes against the person is LEAST likely to be accurate?

A. A male is most likely to be a victim in a major crime against the person (except homicide) when he is on the street.
B. The highest victimization rate for robbery is for males between the ages of 20 and 29.

C. A female is most likely to be a victim in a major crime against the person (except homicide) when she is in her place of residence.
D. An assaultive crime against a white victim is more likely to be committed by a black male than a white male.
E. A very high percentage of the victims of assaults, rapes, and homicides are acquainted with the perpetrator of the crime.

8. Most police administrators recognize the inevitability as well as the benefit of formally organized employee organizations and genuinely want them to function effectively at all levels of their department. This philosophy is best implemented by granting these organizations certain rights and responsibilities when they request them. Which one of the following, if any, is NOT appropriate for a police administrator to grant, despite his desire to cooperate?
The right to

   A. officially petition and send information upward through the chain of command
   B. formally provide representation for all members who are the object of departmental disciplinary action
   C. be made an unofficial part of the downward communication channels within the department
   D. be consulted and to participate bilaterally in departmental policy decisions affecting conditions of employment
   E. None of the above, since it is best to grant all of the above rights before they are demanded.

9. A police administrator should be aware of the landmark decisions of the United States Supreme Court which affect his profession. One of the major areas to which the Court has addressed itself recently is the right to legal counsel.
In which one of the following cases, if any, was the right to legal counsel NOT the primary issue?

   A. Mapp v. Ohio
   B. Miranda v. Arizona
   C. Escobedo v. Illinois
   D. Gideon v. Wainwright
   E. None of the above, since right to legal counsel was the primary issue in each case

10. In 1968, Congress passed the Juvenile Delinquency Prevention and Control Act (Public Law 90-445). This act has significance to police departments and police commanders. Which one of the following is NOT a provision of this act?
Providing funds to support

   A. the relocation of dependent and neglected children
   B. the counseling of the parents of delinquent children
   C. the development of diagnostic techniques to predict delinquency
   D. the development of formal training material on the causes of delinquency
   E. college and university courses for individual police officers through their departments

11. The National Advisory Commission on Civil Disorders has reported that substantial percentages of Blacks in most large cities feel that there is some form of brutality in police dealings within their communities. A survey based on observations of police-citizen contacts in slum precincts in three large cities was conducted to investigate these findings and, while this survey may not fully reflect the normal pattern of police conduct, police commanders should nevertheless be aware of the results.
Which one of the following is LEAST likely to have been observed as fact during this survey?

   A. Only 0.3% of the observed contacts involved excessive or unnecessary physical force.
   B. Almost all of the persons upon whom unnecessary force was observed to be used were poor.
   C. 15% of all contacts observed began with a *brusque or nasty command.*
   D. More blacks than whites are likely to be subjected to verbal discourtesies during police-citizen contacts.
   E. Observations of verbal discourtesies were much more common than observations of excessive or unnecessary force.

11._____

12. Police-press relations and the ability of individual police commanders to deal with the press are important to the proper functioning of a police department.
Which one of the following statements concerning police-press relations is LEAST likely to be accurate?

   A. Most newspapermen feel it is their duty to honor a confidence once it is given to them.
   B. Confessions and admissions made by persons in custody should not be released to the press.
   C. There have been instances of irresponsible action by the press which have increased the difficulty in solving major crimes.
   D. The local press is usually interested only in sensational crime stories and is not concerned with internal police department news such as retirements, transfers, etc.
   E. If a police commander makes too much use of the tactic of giving newsmen *facts to be held in confidence,* the newsmen may begin to reject such information and attempt to find out the facts themselves, so that they will be free to print them.

12._____

13. The term *selective enforcement* has a specific and well-recognized meaning in the police profession. While usually the term is used most often in the area of traffic, this general principle is applicable to all areas of police enforcement work.
Which one of the following actions taken by a police commander is LEAST appropriately called a *selective enforcement* action?

   A. He details a two-man bank stakeout team to set up in banks on Fridays and Saturdays.
   B. He instructs his traffic enforcement men to allow 10% over the speed limit before issuing a summons.
   C. He assigns men in plain clothes to walk streets in areas where there are high incidents of robbery.
   D. He stations a sector car at a specific stop sign controlled intersection between 7:00 A.M. and 8:20 A.M. because of accidents.

13._____

E. When manpower is available, he details sector cars away from routine patrols and assigns them specific speed enforcement responsibility on through streets with high accident frequencies.

14. In a certain police district which has four overlapping shifts, eight patrol cars are assigned to specific beats from 4 P.M. to 12 P.M. Three additional cars are assigned to duty when the 7 P.M. to 3 A.M. shift reports. One of the methods which might be used to assign the 11 cars is, at 7 P.M. to change from eight beats to 11 smaller beats with different boundaries. Another method is to assign the three additional cars to roam the entire district.
Which one of the following is LEAST likely to be a problem in assigning the additional cars to roam?
The supervisor will find

   A. that the problems of follow-up are increased
   B. it is difficult to establish clear responsibility for each beat
   C. that maintaining control of the roaming cars is more difficult
   D. it is almost impossible to avoid confusion as to the exact boundaries of the beats assigned to individual non-roaming cars
   E. that the roaming car may *jump* the more interesting calls, to the detriment of the morale of the men assigned to the beat

14.____

15. Most authorities agree that a sound police-community relations program begins with the individual police officer's knowledge of people.
Which one of the following benefits is MOST harmful to the development of sound police-community relations?
That

   A. all people are ethically equal
   B. people are personally and culturally different
   C. there are many persons whose basic suspicion of police comes from preconditioning by parents
   D. there are many people in our society whose opportunities have been limited because of economic factors
   E. there are very few people in our society whose opportunities have been limited because of socio-economic factors

15.____

16. A modern police supervisor, in a large urban area, should understand some of the factors affecting the Black subculture found in the ghetto areas.
Following are three statements concerning this subculture which might possibly be accurate statements:
   I. Many leading students of the problem, Black and White, feel that both the deterioration of the Black family and its matriarchal structure are at the heart of the problem
   II. The Black female's desire to control the Black family structure has been a major factor in driving the Black male into the street
   III. Black civil rights leaders have enthusiastically supported those studies whose conclusions have been to direct our efforts at improving the structure of the Black family

16.____

Which one of the following choices lists ALL of the above statements that are accurate and NONE that is not?

- A. II is an accurate statement but I and III are not.
- B. II and III are accurate statements but I is not.
- C. I and III are accurate statements but II is not.
- D. I is an accurate statement but II and III are not.
- E. III is an accurate statement but I and II are not.

17. Much has been heard recently about the concept of police-community relations, and many police commanders have developed staff police-community relations officers. Which one of the following MOST accurately represents the basic underlying purpose of a police-community relations program, as it is commonly defined by most police authorities?

    - A. The education of the persons and groups within the community concerning the role of the police
    - B. A transfer of ideas and opinions between the police department and the persons and groups within the community
    - C. The preservation of the *status quo* existing between the various persons and groups within the community
    - D. The prevention of violence between the various persons and groups within the community who possess divergent views
    - E. The enforcement of that concept of law and order held by the majority of persons in the community, upon all of the various radically oriented persons and groups within the community

18. The National Advisory Commission on Civil Disorders made a number of observations on police control of civil disorders which are extremely important to a police commander. Following are three observations that the Commission might possibly have made:

    I. The over-response to an incident, e.g., too much visible force, may tend to aggravate a tense situation
    II. The violence and severity of civil disorders were directly related to the seriousness of the precipitating incident (police shooting a Black suspect, etc.)
    III. The police have lost control of tense situations because of an insufficient number of personnel on hand in the initial stages

    Which one of the following choices lists ALL of the above that were observations of the Commission and NONE that was not?

    - A. I and II were observations but III was not.
    - B. I and III were observations but II was not.
    - C. I, II, and III all were observations.
    - D. II and III were observations but I was not.
    - E. III was an observation but I and II were not.

19. The Task Force report, THE POLICE, recognizes the need for development of policies to guide police officers in handling a wide variety of situations.
    Following are three conclusions which might possibly be accurate, according to the Task Force report:

    I. There has been a general failure of police to develop policies for dealing with crimes and potential crime situations
    II. The greatest deficiency in policy statements is in the area of traffic enforcement and juvenile processing

III. Police departments are much more apt to issue policy statements covering internal management procedures than covering external enforcement situations

Which one of the following choices lists ALL of the above statements that are accurate, according to the Task Force report, and NONE which is not?

A. I is accurate but II and III are not.
B. I and II are accurate but III is not.
C. I and III are accurate but II is not.
D. I, II, and III all are accurate.
E. II and III are accurate but I is not.

20. A certain large city is in the midst of a relatively small, but unfortunately well-publicized, civil disturbance. Policeman P has not been pulled for riot duty and is on routine patrol in a patrol sector somewhat larger than normal. At 1:00 P.M., he heard reports of sniping there, but for the past two hours P has not heard any information on the condition at the disturbance. At 3:00 P.M., he notices Y driving his car at high speed and pulls him over. Y, in a gruff voice, says, *Hey cop, why aren't you handling those rioters instead of bothering me*? P ignores his comment and says, *Sir, may I see your driver's license. You were exceeding the speed limit.* Y, calming down, then asks, *What is the situation in the riot area*? to which P replies, *Everything is quiet now and under control.* P then issues a summons and allows Y to continue on his way.

Which one of the following BEST states the most serious mistake that P made in handling this situation? P should not have

A. made any statement to Y concerning the situation in the riot area
B. ignored Y's insult but should also have cited Y for insulting a police officer
C. bothered to make a speeding stop when the amount of patrol coverage was diminished, due to the disturbance
D. ignored Y's initial affront and should have explained that police patrol was being maintained despite the disturbance
E. told Y that the disturbance was quiet but should have informed him that there are reports of scattered sniping

21. Much has been written about the causes of riots and civil unrest.
Which one of the following widely-held views as to the causes of rioting has actually been found to be ERRONEOUS? There is

A. personal friction among members of the involved community, based on social differences
B. an increase in the consumption of alcoholic beverages by prominent participants in riots
C. a high degree of frustration in finding solutions to problems among prominent participants in riots
D. a breakdown of respect for the police and the government in general, among prominent participants in riots
E. a pathological syndrome in many of the prominent participants in riots in that they act without real underlying causes

22. Following are three general statements on group behavior which the overwhelming weight of evidence might possibly show to be true:
    I. Most judges and social workers are too lenient with juvenile offenders
    II. Generally speaking, people fall into two categories: good or bad
    III. Most men have destructive impulses which must be controlled by society

    Which one of the following choices lists ALL of the above generalities which have been shown to be true and NONE which have not, according to POLICE AND THE CHANGING COMMUNITY?

    A. I has been shown to be true but II and III have not.
    B. I and III have been shown to be true but II has not.
    C. I, II, and III all have been shown to be true.
    D. None of I, II, or III has been shown to be true.
    E. III has been shown to be true but I and II have not.

23. We hear a great deal today about community relations, human relations, public relations, etc. While many of these concepts are similar, there are recognized differences in direction and emphasis.
    Following is a definition of one of these concepts: The development of a favorable public impression of a given product (service), with a tendency often to place more emphasis upon *looking good* than upon *being good*.
    Which one of the following labels is MOST often used to convey the above concept? _____ relations.

    A. Human
    B. Public
    C. Community
    D. Civil rights
    E. Minority group

24. Prejudiced persons are often characterized by what psychiatrists call a weak self-image. They are fearful of their own impulses; they are insecure, become rigid-minded in an attempt to get stability. It then becomes difficult for them to adapt and adjust to the forces of change. This statement was made during a discussion on police professionalism in relationship to police-community relations.
    Which one of the following ideas is it MOST significant for a police commander to understand from the above statement when he analyzes his community relations program?

    A. The importance of the attitude of the minority group members toward themselves
    B. The importance of the attitude of the individual police officer toward himself
    C. A recognition that police officers are actually more prejudiced than majority group members
    D. The importance of the attitude of the individual police officers toward minority group members
    E. A recognition that minority group members are actually more prejudiced than majority group members

25. A certain police commander has to select a man to head up the new community relations unit. A high degree of leadership ability is necessary in this position because a major part of the program involves reorienting the attitudes of men in the department as well as establishing communications between the minority community and the department. He has narrowed his choice to the following three patrolmen, all of whom are of the same race.

A description of the outstanding characteristics of each follows. Other than for the characteristics described, all three are equal.

Patrolman

    I. W has considerable physical vitality and has always worked hard and been industrious. In addition, he has a high tolerance for frustration. He has no significant experience in community relations or in supervision

    II. S is young and tremendously ambitious to create a name for himself. He would literally do anything to make a success of any of his programs. He has had some slight supervisory experience but no community relations experience

    III. P has technical mastery of his job, so that he can give orders forcefully. He is reserved and avoids making personal contacts with his associates. He has had no experience in community relations or supervision

Which one of the following choices BEST evaluates these three candidates for the leadership position of community relations officer, based on the facts given above?

    A. W is clearly better qualified than the others, with P second choice, and S third choice.
    B. P is clearly better qualified than the others, with W second choice, and S third choice.
    C. W and P are probably equally, but differently, qualified, and S is the third choice.
    D. Although each offers different strengths, all three are equally well-qualified for the position.
    E. S is the best qualified, and W or P, although different, are equally acceptable as the second choice.

KEY (CORRECT ANSWERS)

1. D			11. D	
2. E			12. D	
3. B			13. B	
4. E			14. D	
5. A			15. E	
6. A			16. D	
7. D			17. B	
8. E			18. B	
9. A			19. C	
10. A			20. A	

    21. E
    22. D
    23. B
    24. B
    25. A

TEST 2

DIRECTIONS: Each question or incomplete statement is followed by several suggested answers or completions. Select the one that BEST answers the question or completes the statement. *PRINT THE LETTER OF THE CORRECT ANSWER IN THE SPACE AT THE RIGHT.*

1. Which one of the following should a police commander recognize as being the policy TRULY at the heart of a police-community relations program?
An enforced

   A. operational policy of equal treatment for all members of the community
   B. operational policy of equal enforcement of all laws imposed on the community
   C. organizational policy of establishing the staff function of community relations at the precinct level
   D. operational policy of matching whenever possible the ethnic background of police officers to the communities where they are assigned to patrol
   E. personnel policy of equal job opportunities and promotional opportunities for all religious, racial, language, and other groups within the community and the department

1.____

2. A police commander should be aware of the nature of the various organizations that represent or purport to represent minority groups in large cities.
The following is a brief description of one such organization: It is something more than a religious organization concerned with reforming the existing social order. At a minimum, they want a separate order in an autonomous society; and ideally, they anticipate a reversal of the existing caste arrangements in the existing order of this society.
Which one of the following is MOST likely to be the organization described above?

   A. CORE
   B. The NAACP
   C. The Black Muslims
   D. The Black Panthers
   E. The John Birch Society

2.____

3. A very important dilemma in law enforcement is that some persons feel strongly that crime among minority groups ought to be stamped out, even at a high cost in the violation of civil liberties; others feel that civil liberties ought to be safeguarded, even at a high cost in crime.
Which one of the following BEST states who, in the long run, must be given final responsibility for solving this dilemma?

   A. The courts
   B. The individual beat patrolman
   C. Police commanders, at precinct and higher levels
   D. The community itself, through its legislature
   E. The leadership of those organizations that truly represent the minorities

3.____

4. Following are four statements concerning the assignment of police personnel to speak before community groups that might possibly be appropriate as guidelines for a police commander:
   I. A police department should resist use of its members as speakers and provide them only when it is absolutely necessary
   II. When a speaker is approved, the topic or subject of the speech should be dictated by the interests and wishes of the group requesting the speaker
   III. In large departments, a public contact bureau or similar unit should be developed to match up speakers and groups

4.____

IV. All members of a police department should be prohibited from making any speeches without the express approval of the department

Which one of the following choices lists ALL of the above statements that are appropriate and NONE that is not?

A. II and III are appropriate but I and IV are not.
B. I is appropriate but II, III, and IV are not.
C. I and IV are appropriate but II and III are not.
D. III is appropriate but I, II, and IV are not.
E. II and IV are appropriate but I and III are not.

5. A certain student of law enforcement has made the comment that it does not take great reflection to understand that, by permitting the police to use criminal tactics, we could not decrease the problem of crime—we increase it. No segment of the population, not the law enforcers, not even police commanders, can be permitted to flout the law. This statement was made as a rebuttal to a complaint frequently made by police commanders.
Which one of the following is MOST likely this complaint?

A. Local courts are unable to make appropriate decisions in light of recent Supreme Court decisions.
B. The Supreme Court has greatly restricted the types of enforcement practices that the police can employ.
C. The increased professionalization and knowledge level of the habitual criminal makes many police efforts ineffective.
D. Police conditions encourage individual patrolmen to become corrupt and protect vice activities at the local beat level.
E. It is difficult to determine when the police have the right to arrest, for breach of the peace, during civil rights and other demonstrations.

6. A police commander is judged by many standards, such as the crime rate in his area, his arrest and clearance rates, and, to a lesser extent, his conviction rate. Many feel that the crime of aggravated assault should produce a high rate of arrest and conviction. Yet this is not the case, especially in the ghetto areas of large cities. Even when large numbers of these cases are reported to the police, in many instances no arrest is made or, if one is made, no prosecution is attempted.
Which one of the following is the MOST serious problem police commanders experience in regard to the successful processing of a reported aggravated assault? The

A. unwillingness of the courts to accept hearsay testimony
B. fact that no police officers have actually observed the crime
C. fact that the victim is often unwilling to cooperate with the police
D. rigid restrictions placed by the courts on the use of confessions
E. fact that the perpetrator of the crime is seldom known to the victim

7. There is much concern about the types of crimes committed by juvenile gang members. Which one of the following, according to Kenny and Pursuit in POLICE WORK WITH JUVENILES, BEST states the types of crimes committed most frequently by juveniles and which very often account for up to 25% of all juvenile gang crimes?

A. Assaults
B. Drug Use
C. Vandalism
D. Auto theft
E. Thefts (excluding auto theft)

8. Which one of the following is the MOST common *direct* cause of death due to narcotics overdosage, as opposed to deaths caused *indirectly* by narcotics usage?

   A. Hepatitis
   B. Heart damage
   C. Brain abcesses
   D. Blood poisoning
   E. Respiratory depression

9. The recent upsurge in juvenile delinquency problems has prompted efforts to find methods of predicting who will become delinquent.
   Which one of the following is the MOST important benefit that can be derived from the ability to make this prediction?
   Ability to

   A. recognize the family structures that create the highest incidence of delinquency
   B. analyze different environmental factors as they relate to juvenile crime and delinquency
   C. recognize potential juvenile delinquents before they commit delinquent acts, in order to take them out of their environment and place them in special schools
   D. deploy police enforcement efforts in those areas where juvenile crime is most likely to be committed
   E. concentrate programs designed to prevent delinquency toward those persons most seriously in need of such efforts

10. A certain police department is contemplating using evidence technicians, according to the procedures recommended by O.W. Wilson in his book, POLICE ADMINISTRATION. Following are three statements that might possibly be in accordance with Wilson's recommendations:

    I. The evidence technician shall be assigned directly to the patrol function and receive his direct supervision from patrol supervisors
    II. The evidence technician shall be responsible only for the collection and preservation of physical evidence. The task of searching crime scenes should remain the responsibility of the investigating detective or beat patrolman.
    III. The evidence technician shall be responsible for performing work at both crime scenes and accident scenes

    Which one of the following choices lists ALL of the above statements that are recommended by Wilson and NONE that is not?

    A. I is recommended by Wilson but II and III are not.
    B. I and II are recommended by Wilson but III is not.
    C. I and III are recommended by Wilson but II is not.
    D. I, II, and III all are recommended by Wilson.
    E. III is recommended by Wilson but I and II are not.

11. Crime clearance is an important problem confronting police.
    Following are three statements concerning the solution of crimes which may possibly be accurate:

    I. A single latent fingerprint is almost useless when there are no suspects to the crime
    II. The percentage of crimes which are cleared without a suspect being named by a witness usually is significantly below 20%
    III. If a suspect is not in custody within two hours after a crime has been committed, the chances of clearance decrease

Which one of the following choices lists ALL of the above statements that are accurate and NONE that is not?

- A. I and II are accurate statements but III is not.
- B. I and III are accurate statements but II is not.
- C. I, II, and III all are accurate statements.
- D. II and III are accurate statements but I is not.
- E. III is an accurate statement but I and II are not.

12. Police commanders in large jurisdictions have had serious problems with juvenile gangs. POLICE WORK WITH JUVENILES reports on a study of juvenile gangs which appears to be appropriate for most large city gangs. This study has exploded some popular beliefs about gang leadership.
Which one of the following beliefs on gang leadership is MOST likely to have been exploded?
Gang

- A. leadership usually falls to members of the gang who are noted for their *cool* behavioral style
- B. leadership tends to fluctuate among various persons depending upon the gang activities in question
- C. leadership usually falls to members of the gang who are able to bring benefits to the group
- D. leadership tends to fall to those individuals with psychopathic tendencies (emotionally disturbed) owing to their aggressive behavioral patterns
- E. membership is usually stratified by age group and younger members are influenced more by their peers than by the admired leaders of the oldest age group

13. A certain police commander, confronted with a high incidence of commercial breakings and enterings, instituted a program of *door shaking*. He determined that there were 7,098 store doors which, under his policy, were to be checked twice each night. A year later, his records disclosed that in the first year of the program, patrolmen found only 970 store doors unlocked. In other words, if police patrolled in accordance with policy, there should have been about 5,200,000 door shakes that year or one open premise for about every 12,000 *shakes*.
Based on this information, which one of the following is the MOST appropriate decision for a commander to make? To

- A. continue the *door shaking* policy as it is presently constituted without any change
- B. discontinue the *door shaking* policy entirely and distribute all of these man-hours to routine patrol
- C. request additional manpower from his superior, so as to be able to maintain the *door shaking* procedure
- D. modify his *door shaking* policy so as not to include all business places, but only a certain, much smaller percentage selected through analysis
- E. continue the *door shaking* policy and to instruct his field supervisors to follow behind the men shaking doors in order to ascertain whether they are actually finding all the unsecure doors which exist

14. Following are three statements on the serious juvenile delinquency crime problem that might possibly be accurate:
    I. There is a greater proportion of unreported delinquency and juvenile crime in middle-class areas as compared to lower socio-economic areas
    II. There is a real and meaningful difference in the amount and type of juvenile crime committed in lower socio-economic areas as compared to middle-class areas
    III. When factors of religion, nationality, and race are held constant and the factor *where one is growing up* is the only variable, then delinquency rates are constant

    Which one of the following choices lists ALL of the above statements that are accurate and NONE that is not?

    A. I and II are accurate statements but III is not.
    B. I and III are accurate statements but II is not.
    C. I, II, and III all are accurate statements.
    D. Neither I, II, nor III is an accurate statement.
    E. II is an accurate statement but I and III are not.

15. A statement often heard in law enforcement lately is that, based on arrest statistics, which admittedly is only a rough measure, youths (juveniles) are apparently responsible for a substantial and disproportionate part of the national crime problem.
    Which one of the following is the MOST accurate evaluation of this statement?

    A. It is most probably incorrect, since juveniles are more easily arrested than adults.
    B. It is most probably true and grossly understated, because a large percentage of juvenile arrests is not recorded.
    C. It is most probably incorrect, because juveniles usually operate in groups, thus producing large numbers of juvenile arrests.
    D. It is most probably incorrect, because the definition of a juvenile, in terms of age, is much more restricted than the definition of an adult.
    E. While probably slightly exaggerated, it is most probably true because persons between the ages of 15 and 20 are involved in a disproportionate number of crimes.

16. While on duty, P, a police officer, received from his superior a description of Z, who was involved in a robbery and believed to be in P's area. The superior officer's information concerning Z's involvement in the robbery came from a reliable third party. P observes a person closely matching Z's description. When P approaches, the person starts to run, but is quickly apprehended and placed under arrest for robbery. While searching this person for weapons, P discovers a quantity of narcotics in his inside coat pocket and forthwith seizes the narcotics.
    Which one of the following MOST properly evaluates both whether or not the seizure of the narcotics was proper in this case, and also the BEST reason therefor?
    The seizure was

    A. *proper,* but only because narcotics are contraband
    B. *proper,* since it was made incident to a lawful arrest
    C. *improper,* since P did not have an arrest warrant for Z
    D. *improper,* since P did not have probable cause for arrest
    E. *improper,* since the narcotics were unrelated to the crime for which the arrest was made

17. Following are three situations in which *Miranda* warnings were not given when the confessions made by the persons involved might possibly be admissible as evidence:
A person
    I. walks into a police station and volunteers a statement to the desk sergeant, implicating himself in a robbery
    II. in prison for committing a certain crime, being questioned concerning his involvement in a second crime, confesses to the second crime
    III. arrested at the scene of a robbery attempt, being questioned concerning the crime, confesses to the crime

    Which one of the following choices lists ALL of the above situations in which the confession is admissible and NONE in which it is not?
    The confession is admissible in

    A. I but not in II and III
    B. I and II but not in III
    C. I, II, and III
    D. I and III but not in II
    E. III but not in I and II

18. R forcibly stole property from Z.
    Which one of the following additional elements, if present, would MOST properly justify charging R with robbery in the first degree, rather than robbery in the third degree?

    A. R punched Z during the robbery, giving Z a black eye.
    B. R used a motor vehicle to escape from the robbery scene.
    C. R was aided by an accomplice when committing the robbery.
    D. R produced a knife and threatened to use it, but did not stab Z, when committing the robbery.
    E. R produced a gun and threatened to use it during the robbery. The gun was unloaded but Z did not know this.

19. Patrolman P, having received information from a reliable third party that Z had committed a misdemeanor, arrests Z without a warrant and drives him to the lockup. As Z is being transferred from the patrol car to the lockup, he breaks away from P and runs into a crowd of persons. After a ten-minute foot chase, P reapprehends Z.
    Which one of the following BEST states the offense or offenses, if any, for which P may now properly arrest Z without a warrant?

    A. Only escape in the third degree
    B. Only escape in the second degree
    C. Only the misdemeanor for which he was originally arrested
    D. P may not properly arrest Z for any of the above offenses
    E. The misdemeanor for which he was originally arrested and escape in the third degree

20. A stolen car with three occupants is stopped after a highspeed chase and the occupants are arrested. P, one of the occupants, has an unloaded, but operable, .32 caliber pistol tucked in his belt, and six .32 caliber rounds in his pocket. U, the second occupant, has an unloaded, but operable, .45 caliber pistol in his pants' pocket and has no bullets on his person. L, the driver, has neither a pistol nor any ammunition on his person. When the vehicle is searched, a loaded .38 caliber pistol is found under the right front seat. None of the occupants of the car has ever been convicted of a crime, and none has a valid license for any of the weapons.
    Which one of the following BEST states which weapon or weapons each man may PROPERLY be charged with felonious possession of?

A. P, U, and L may each properly be charged with felonious possession of only the .32 and the .38.
B. P, U, and L may each properly be charged with felonious possession of the .32, the .38, and the .45.
C. P may properly be charged only with felonious possession of the .32, and both U and L may not be properly charged with the felonious possession of any of the weapons.
D. P may properly be charged with felonious possession of only the .32, U may properly be charged only with the felonious possession of the .45, and L may not be properly charged with the felonious possession of any of the weapons.
E. P may properly be charged with felonious possession only of the .32 and the .38, U may properly be charged with felonious possession only of the .45 and the .38, and L may properly be charged with felonious possession only of the .38.

21. Following are three situations in which a police officer might possibly be justified in using DEADLY physical force upon another person:
    I. To prevent the escape of an unarmed person who was seen by the officer snatching a woman's purse
    II. To arrest an unarmed person observed by the officer committing arson
    III. To arrest an unarmed person when the officer reasonably believes that the person is likely to inflict serious physical injury on a third party unless apprehended without delay, under conditions that do not amount to imminent use of deadly physical force
    Which one of the following choices lists ALL of the above cases in which a police officer is actually justified in using DEADLY physical force and NONE in which he is not?
    He is

    A. justified in I, II, and III
    B. not justified in I, II, or III
    C. justified in I and III, but not in II
    D. justified in II but not in I and III
    E. justified in II and III but not in I

21._____

22. L lends R a pistol, believing that R intends to use the pistol to rob V. During the robbery, with which L had no further part, R kills V.
    Which one of the following, if any, is the MOST serious crime with which L may properly be charged?

    A. Conspiracy in the fourth degree
    B. Criminal facilitation in the first degree
    C. Criminal facilitation in the second degree
    D. Criminal solicitation in the second degree
    E. None of the above, since he may not properly be charged with any crime

22._____

23. Which one of the following is LEAST likely to be a degree-raising factor for the crime of assault?
That

   A. a dangerous instrument was used
   B. the assailant was over 18 years of age when the assault occurred
   C. *serious physical injury* rather than *ordinary physical injury* was caused
   D. physical injury was caused intentionally rather than recklessly
   E. physical injury was inflicted in the course of the commission of an independent felony

23.____

24. R and S, while planning an armed robbery of an armored truck, study the route taken by the truck from a bank to a factory where payroll money is delivered every Thursday. A bartender hears their conversation and informs the police. Part of the plan involves staging an automobile accident along the route taken by the truck, and robbing the truck when the driver stops.
On the day of the intended robbery, the route taken by the truck is altered so that it will not pass by the location where R and S have staged the accident and R and S, both heavily armed, are arrested by police at the scene.
Which one of the following is the MOST serious crime with which R and S may properly be charged?
_____ in the _____ degree.

   A. Robbery; first
   B. Conspiracy; third
   C. Conspiracy; second
   D. Attempted robbery; first
   E. Attempted robbery; second

24.____

25. Recently, the section of the State Penal Law dealing with murder was modified in several respects. One such modification concerned an aspect of the *felony murder* doctrine of the Law.
Which one of the following is both the MOST accurate statement as to how the felony murder doctrine was modified and also the APPARENT LEGISLATIVE INTENT therefor?

   A. Listing certain specific felonies, to clarify the meaning of the term *any felony* in the former statute
   B. Including all felonies under the felony murder doctrine, so that a fatality which occurs during the commission of any felony is punishable as murder
   C. Including all felonies in which a motor vehicle is used, either in committing the felony or in escaping from the scene, so that fatalities which occur in these cases are punishable as murder
   D. Excluding certain non-violent felonies from the felony murder doctrine, so that a fatality which is either accidental or which the perpetrator cannot reasonably foresee, is not punishable as murder
   E. Adding the necessity of proving intent as an element of murder in non-violent felonies, so that a fatality in connection with a non-violent felony is not punishable as murder when intent cannot be proved

25.____

KEY (CORRECT ANSWERS)

1. A
2. C
3. D
4. A
5. B

6. C
7. E
8. E
9. E
10. C

11. C
12. D
13. D
14. A
15. E

16. B
17. A
18. D
19. D
20. A

21. D
22. C
23. B
24. D
25. D

READING COMPREHENSION
UNDERSTANDING AND INTERPRETING WRITTEN MATERIAL

EXAMINATION SECTION
TEST 1

DIRECTIONS: Each question or incomplete statement is followed bpy several suggested answers or completions. Select the one that BEST answers the question or completes the statement. *PRINT THE LETTER OF THE CORRECT ANSWER IN THE SPACE AT THE RIGHT.*

Questions 1-4.

DIRECTIONS: Questions 1 through 4 are to be answered on the basis of the following passage.

It should be emphasized that one goal of law enforcement is the reduction of stress between one population group and another. When no stress exists between populations, law enforcement can deal with other tensions or simply perform traditional police functions. However, when stress between populations does exist, law enforcement, in its efforts to prevent disruptive behavior, becomes committed to reducing that stress (if for no other reason than its responsibility to maintain an orderly environment). The type of stress to be reduced, unlike the tension stemming from social change, is stress generated through intergroup and interracial friction. Of course, all sources of tension are inextricably interrelated, but friction between different populations in the community is of immediate concern to law enforcement.

1. The above passage emphasizes that, during times of stress between groups in the community, it is necessary for the police to attempt to

    A. continue their traditional duties
    B. eliminate tension resulting from social change
    C. reduce intergroup stress
    D. punish disruptive behavior

2. Based on the above passage, police concern with tension among groups in a community is MOST likely to stem primarily from their desire to

    A. establish racial justice
    B. prevent violence
    C. protect property
    D. unite the diverse groups

3. According to the above passage, enforcers of the law are responsible for

    A. analyzing consequences of population-group hostility
    B. assisting social work activities
    C. creating order in the environment
    D. explaining group behavior

4. The factor which produces the tension accompanying social change is 4.____

   A. a disorderly environment
   B. disruptive behavior
   C. inter-community hostility
   D. not discussed in the above passage

Questions 5-7.

DIRECTIONS: Questions 5 through 7 are to be answered SOLELY on the basis of the following paragraphs.

Perhaps the most difficult administrative problem of the police records unit is the maintenance of cooperative relationships with the operating units in the department. Unless these relationships are completely accepted by the operating units, some records activities will result in friction. The records system is a tool of the chief administrative officer and the various supervising officers in managing personnel, police operations, and procedures. However, the records unit must constantly check on the records activities of all members of the department if the records system is to serve as a really effective tool for these supervisory officers.

The first step in avoiding conflict between the records and the operating units is to develop definite policies and regulations governing the records system. These regulations should be prepared jointly by the head of the records unit and the heads of the operating units under the leadership of the chief administrative officer of the department. Once the records policies and regulations have been agreed upon, the task is to secure conformity. Theoretically, if a patrolman fails to prepare a report of an investigation, his commanding officer should be notified by the records unit and he, in turn, should take appropriate measures to secure the report. Practically, this line of command must be cut across in the case of such routine matters, or the commanding officer will spend time in keeping the records system going that should be devoted to the other police duties which comprise the major work of the department. However, if the patrolman is persistently negligent, or if a new policy or procedure is being initiated, the records unit must deal through the commanding officer.

5. According to the above passage, the one of the following situations in which the records unit would MOST likely contact a commanding officer of an operating unit is when 5.____

   A. a patrolman has expressed disagreement with a records unit policy and suggests a modification of the policy
   B. an important report, which involves more than one operating unit, has been carelessly prepared by a patrolman
   C. the commanding officer of the operating unit devotes little time to police duties which comprise the major work of the department
   D. the records unit has received orders from the chief administrative officer to institute several changes in previous records procedures

6. According to the above paragraph, obtaining agreement as to definite policies, and regulations governing the records system 6.____

   A. guarantees the avoidance of conflict between the records and operating divisions
   B. is of lesser importance than the maintenance of cooperative relationships thereafter

C. should precede any active records division efforts to gain compliance with such policies and regulations
D. should be preceded by an evaluation of the extent to which supervisory officers consider the system an effective management tool

7. According to the above passage, conflict between the records division and the operating divisions is MOST likely to result when the

A. chief administrative officer denies to the records division the authority to check on the records activities of all members of the department
B. operating divisions are not convinced that their work contacts with the records division are useful and desirable
C. records division voluntarily attempts to establish productive relationships with operating divisions
D. operating divisions understand the specific nature i of records division duties

7.____

Questions 8-10.

DIRECTIONS: Questions 8 through 10 are to be answered SOLELY on the basis of the following paragraph.

Early in the development of police service, legislators granted powers and authority to policemen beyond their inherent rights as citizens in order that they would be able to act effectively in the discharge of their duties. The law makers also recognized the fact that unless policemen were excused from complete obedience to certain laws and regulations, they would be seriously encumbered in the effective discharge of their duties. The exemptions were specifically provided for by legislative action because of the danger of abuse of power involved in granting blanket privileges and powers. The public, however, has not been so discriminating and has gone well beyond the law in excusing policemen from full obedience to regulatory measures. The liberal interpretation that the public has placed upon the right of police officers to disobey the law has been motivated in part by public confidence in law enforcement and in part by a sincere desire of the public to assist the police in every way in the performance of their duties. Further, the average citizen is not interested in the technicalities of law enforcement nor is he aware of the legal limitations that are placed upon the authority of policemen. It is a regrettable fact that many policemen assume so-called rights of law that either do not exist or that are subject to well-defined legal limitations, because the public generally is unaware of the limitations placed by law upon policemen.

8. According to the above paragraph, the one of the following statements which BEST explains the reason for granting special legal powers to policemen is that such powers are granted

A. because the exercise of their inherent rights by citizens frequently conflicted with efficient law enforcement
B. because the public has not been sufficiently vigilant in objecting to blanket grants of power
C. in order to excuse policemen from full obedience to laws and regulations which they are unable to enforce
D. in order to remove certain handicaps experienced by policemen in law enforcement operations

8.____

9. According to the above paragraph, specific legislative exemptions for policemen from complete obedience to certain laws and regulations

   A. are based largely on so-called rights of law that either do not exist or are misinterpreted by the public
   B. have not been abused by the police even though most individual policemen ignore proper legal limitations
   C. have not provided a fully effective limitation on the exercise of unwarranted police authority
   D. have been misunderstood by the police and the public partly because they are based on unduly technical laws

10. According to the above paragraph, the one of the following statements which BEST explains the liberal attitude of the public toward the special powers of policemen is that the public

    A. believes that the police are justified in disregarding the technicalities of law enforcement and also wants to assist the police in the performance of their duties
    B. feels that the laws restricting police authority are overly strict and also believes that the police are performing their duties in a proper manner
    C. is not aware of the legal restrictions on police authority and also believes that the police are performing their duties in a proper manner
    D. wants to assist the police in the performance of their duties and also feels that the laws on police authority are sufficiently restrictive

Questions 11-12.

DIRECTIONS: Questions 11 and 12 are to be answered SOLELY on the basis of the following paragraph.

The personal conduct of each member of the department is the primary factor in promoting desirable police-community relations. Tact, patience, and courtesy shall be strictly observed under all circumstances. A favorable public attitude toward the police must be earned; it is influenced by the personal conduct and attitude of each member of the force; by his personal integrity and courteous manner; by his respect for due process of law; by his devotion to the principles of justice, fairness, and impartiality.

11. According to the above paragraph, what is the BEST action an officer can take in dealing with people in a neighborhood?

    A. Assist neighborhood residents by doing favors for them
    B. Give special attention to the community leaders in order to be able to control them effectively
    C. Behave in an appropriate manner and give all community members the same just treatment
    D. Prepare a plan detailing what he, the officer, wants to do for the community and submit it for approval

12. As used in the above paragraph, the word impartiality means MOST NEARLY

    A. observant   B. unbiased
    C. righteousness D. honesty

Questions 13-16.

DIRECTIONS: Questions 13 through 16 are to be answered on the basis of the information given in the following passage.

The public often believes that the main job of a uniformed officer is to enforce laws by simply arresting people. In reality, however, many of the situations that an officer deals with do not call for the use of his arrest power. In the first place, an officer spends much of his time preventing crimes from happening, by spotting potential violations or suspicious behavior and taking action to prevent illegal acts. In the second place, many of the situations in which officers are called on for assistance involve elements like personal arguments, husband-wife quarrels, noisy juveniles, or mentally disturbed persons. The majority of these problems do not result in arrests and convictions, and often they do not even involve illegal behavior. In the third place, even in situations where there seems to be good reason to make an arrest, an officer may have to exercise very good judgment. There are times when making an arrest too soon could touch off a riot, or could result in the detention of a minor offender while major offenders escaped, or could cut short the gathering of necessary on-the-scene evidence.

13. The above passage IMPLIES that most citizens

    A. will start to riot if they see an arrest being made
    B. appreciate the work that law enforcement officers do
    C. do not realize that making arrests is only a small part of law enforcement
    D. never call for assistance unless they are involved in a personal argument or a husband-wife quarrel

14. According to the above passage, one way in which law enforcement officers can prevent crimes for happening is by

    A. arresting suspicious characters
    B. letting minor offenders go free
    C. taking action on potential violations
    D. refusing to get involved in husband-wife fights

15. According to the above passage, which of the following statements is NOT true of situations involving mentally disturbed persons?

    A. It is a waste of time to call on law enforcement officers for assistance in such situations.
    B. Such situations may not involve illegal behavior.
    C. Such situations often do not result in arrests.
    D. Citizens often turn to law enforcement officers for help in such situations.

16. The last sentence in the passage mentions *detention of minor offenders*.
    Of the following, which BEST explains the meaning of the word *detention* as used here?

    A. Sentencing someone
    B. Indicting someone
    C. Calling someone before a grand jury
    D. Arresting someone

Questions 17-18.

DIRECTIONS: Questions 17 and 18 are to be answered SOLELY on the basis of the following paragraph.

In order that the police officer can function in a role that is outside the area of his personal prejudices, it is necessary to develop in him a real sense of professionalism. Policing is increasingly recognized as requiring a high degree of technical knowledge and skill. This, however, is only one mark of a profession. Another is the increasing emphasis upon public duty and service to the community. The time has long passed in enlightened police circles when a man became an officer of the law by merely donning a uniform and flashing a star. Training, dedication, and understanding are the cornerstones of modern police science. The police officer must become increasingly aware of the role he plays as a symbol of society's authority - aware that only by examining the relation of his personal sentiments and feelings to his public duties can he achieve true impartiality and neutrality. This is an educational problem in its own right, and it is equal in importance to the acquisition of new information as to the technicalities of crime detection.

17. According to the above paragraph,

    A. the achievement of true neutrality in law enforcement is the most important problem facing the police officer
    B. the emphasis on community service is one of the characteristics of a profession that is being increasingly stressed as a part of police work
    C. the emphasis on the technicalities of crime detection is improper if it detracts from the need of the police to be a symbol of society's authority
    D. technical training is an area of police work which has always received recognition as an important aspect of police science

18. According to the above paragraph,

    A. a consideration of the distinguishing characteristics of other professions leads to the conclusion that police work is not a profession
    B. concern for impartiality in law enforcement has always characterized police administration
    C. the absence of personal prejudice in a police officer determines his effectiveness
    D. the police officer should aim to achieve impartiality by examining his personal sentiments and prejudices, since he serves as a symbol of society's authority

Questions 19-22.

DIRECTIONS: Questions 19 through 22 are to be answered on the basis of the following paragraph.

During actual pursuit of a traffic offender and particularly in speed cases when the operator of the police vehicle is maneuvering for clocking, there is a need for haste so that the clocking may be applied when the motorist is traveling in violation of the speed laws. However, necessary haste cannot include rashness. The pursuit, for whatever purpose, must not be at the expense of the safety of other users of the road. When changing lanes to get ahead, the police operator must do it safely or not at all. Giving proper and clear signals as to his intentions is a must but should not be construed as a guarantee of completing the maneuver safely. He must use good judgment in determining whether his *S* pass can be made safely. If there is a possibility that the motorist to be passed would be forced to apply his brakes to avoid a collision, the passing should be delayed. Instead, he should be notified by hand signal of the police vehicle operator's intention to pass and directed to reduce speed so that the police vehicle can be driven past safely. In other than emergencies, sudden stops should be avoided. In a situation where law enforcement needs require a sudden reduction in speed, consideration must be given to the vehicles behind to preclude rear-end collisions. A gradual reduction in speed, coupled with a sufficient warning to convey the intention to stop or turn is the preferential course of action. Similarly, if at all possible, the police operator should avoid turning at locations that are clearly unfavorable for turning, such as through safety zones or between stanchions placed to prohibit passage, since such maneuvers increase the probability of an accident.

19. The one of the following which MOST adequately describes the central theme of the paragraph is the _____ motorized traffic offenders. 19.____

    A. essentiality of maintaining maximum speed during the pursuit of
    B. danger of passing intervening vehicles while pursuing
    C. precautions to take in the pursuit of
    D. methods of attaining greater speed while pursuing

20. According to the above paragraph, when the operator of a police vehicle is pursuing an offender in the same lane, and approaches another vehicle which is between him and the offender's vehicle, it would be MOST correct to state that the operator of the police vehicle 20.____

    A. may attempt to by-pass the vehicle between him and the offender with complete safety so long as he has given proper and clear automatic and hand signals to its operator
    B. may attempt to by-pass the vehicle between him and the offender even if it would be necessary for him to make an *S* pass to do so
    C. must not attempt to by-pass the vehicle between him and the offender until he has directed its operator to reduce speed
    D. must not attempt to by-pass the vehicle between him and the offender unless he can do so safely without leaving the lane

21. According to the above paragraph, when the operator of a police vehicle notices a motorist driving along and suspects that the motorist may have just violated some traffic law, he MAY 21.____

    A. not exceed the posted speed limit except when he is attempting to get into position to clock the offender's speed
    B. travel at whatever speed he deems necessary in order to catch up with and clock the speeding suspect but only as long as both remain in the same lane and the lane remains clear
    C. not exceed the posted speed limit unless he feels certain that the offender has exceeded or can be reasonably expected to exceed the posted speed limit
    D. exceed the posted speed limit in order to apprehend the violator but must never do so if there is any possibility of danger to anyone else using the road

22. A police vehicle is in pursuit of a motorized traffic offender who is attempting to evade capture by alternating between weaving in and out of slower-moving traffic, making sudden stops, and going through safety zones or stanchions placed to prohibit passage.
According to the above paragraph, the operator in pursuit should GENERALLY

   A. follow right behind the offender through all these maneuvers but keep alert for sudden changes in tactics
   B. avoid engaging in such of these maneuvers as he can without increasing the distance between him and the offender
   C. refrain from engaging in driving maneuvers similar to the offender's without duly considering the inherent dangers
   D. anticipate the offender's actions and take the steps necessary to cut him off when he emerges from safety zones

22.____

23. Citizens understand in a vague and general way that their civil liberties must be respected by the police, but they do not appreciate that this protection necessarily extends both to those who consider themselves to be law observers and to those who are law violators.
The MOST important deduction to be made from this by a police officer is that

   A. public opinion is uninformed and hence may be disregarded
   B. the basis is laid for serious misunderstanding between the police and the public
   C. the public attitude toward severe arrest procedures depends on the personal character of the arrestee and not the crime charged
   D. the public favors a policy of selective law enforcement

23.____

Questions 24-25.

DIRECTIONS: Questions 24 and 25 are to be answered on the basis of the following paragraph.

The most significant improvements in personnel selection procedures can be expected from a program designed to obtain more precise statements of the requirements for a particular position and from the development of procedures that will make it possible to select not just those applicants who are generally best, but those whose abilities and personal characteristics provide the closest fit to the specific job requirement.

24. According to the above paragraph, better personnel selection procedures will result from

   A. simplification of job description
   B. better recruiting procedures
   C. obtaining more detailed experience data from applicants
   D. detailed statements of training and skills required for positions

24.____

25. According to the above paragraph, the MOST desirable applicant for a position is

   A. the one who has all the necessary training, even though he lacks the necessary personal characteristics
   B. the one whose abilities and personal characteristics are of the highest order
   C. generally not the same as the best qualified person
   D. the one whose qualifications are most nearly the same as the job requirement

25.____

KEY (CORRECT ANSWERS)

1.	C	11.	C
2.	B	12.	B
3.	C	13.	C
4.	D	14.	C
5.	D	15.	A
6.	C	16.	D
7.	B	17.	B
8.	D	18.	D
9.	C	19.	C
10.	C	20.	B

21. D
22. C
23. B
24. D
25. D

TEST 2

DIRECTIONS: Each question or incomplete statement is followed by several suggested answers or completions. Select the one that BEST answers the question or completes the statement. *PRINT THE LETTER OF THE CORRECT ANSWER IN THE SPACE AT THE RIGHT.*

Questions 1-3.

DIRECTIONS: Questions 1 through 3 are to be answered SOLELY on the basis of the following paragraph.

Every organization needs a systematic method of checking its operation as a means to increase efficiency and promote economy. Many successful private firms have instituted a system of audits or internal inspections to accomplish these ends. Law enforcement organizations, which have an extremely important service to *sell,* should be no less zealous in developing efficiency and economy in their operations. Periodic, organized, and systematic inspections are one means of promoting the achievement of these objectives. The necessity of an organized inspection system is perhaps greatest in those law enforcement groups which have grown to such a size that the principal officer can no longer personally supervise or be cognizant of every action taken. Smooth and effective operation demands that the head of the organization have at hand some tool with which he can study and enforce general policies and procedures and also direct compliance with day-to-day orders, most of which are put into execution outside his sight and hearing. A good inspection system can serve as that tool.

1. The central thought of the above paragraph is that a system of inspections within a police department   1._____

   A. is unnecessary for a department in which the principal officer can personally supervise all official actions taken
   B. should be instituted at the first indication that there is any deterioration in job performance by the force
   C. should be decentralized and administered by first-line supervisory officers
   D. is an important aid to the police administrator in the accomplishment of law enforcement objectives

2. The MOST accurate of the following statements concerning the need for an organized inspection system in a law enforcement organization is: 2._____
   It is

   A. never needed in an organization of small size where the principal officer can give personal supervision
   B. most needed where the size of the organization prevents direct supervision by the principal officer
   C. more needed in law enforcement organizations than in private firms
   D. especially needed in an organization about to embark upon a needed expansion of services

3. According to the above paragraph, the head of the police organization utilizes the internal inspection system

   A. as a tool which must be constantly re-examined in the light of changing demands for police service
   B. as an administrative technique to increase efficiency and promote economy
   C. by personally visiting those areas of police operation which are outside his sight and hearing
   D. to augment the control of local commanders over detailed field operations

Questions 4-6.

DIRECTIONS: Questions 4 through 6 are to be answered SOLELY on the basis of the following paragraph.

Every officer in a department, from the chief of police to the new recruit, should participate if a human relations program is to be effective. The policies, programs, and examples which the chief initiates become the guide for action by all other officers. Through the command group, lieutenants and above in rank, the chief disseminates throughout the department his policies and ideas for application. It is that group which in essence holds control over a department. Implementation of a human relations program must always be through them, with their full support and understanding obtained. They are the link between the sergeants and the chief; they train and assist the sergeants in all operations and give up some of their authority so the sergeants may have freedom to act. The police sergeant is probably the key to success of any police human relations program, since it is his responsibility to develop a wholesome and loyal attitude in the policemen toward their job, themselves, and toward other officers in the department. Instilling of job satisfaction in the patrolmen becomes his responsibility. If changes are to be made in departmental practices or procedures, it is the sergeant's job to change the policemen's attitudes and to condition them for the change.

4. According to this paragraph, one of the responsibilities of a sergeant is to

   A. inform the command group of any changes in attitude on the part of the policemen
   B. inform the command group of needed changes in practices and procedures and inform the policemen of accomplishments and problems of the command group
   C. insist upon a demonstration of job satisfaction by the policemen
   D. prepare the policemen to accept any impending changes in departmental procedure

5. According to this paragraph, the MOST accurate of the following statements concerning a police human relations program is:

   A. Application of policies and ideas is less the responsibility of the sergeant than of the command group
   B. Newly appointed patrolmen should not participate in a human relations program until the sergeant has had an opportunity to change their attitudes
   C. The key to a successful human relations program is the patrolmen's acceptance of basic departmental procedures
   D. The human relations program can never be successful without being actively supported by the lieutenants

6. According to this paragraph, the command group 6.____
   A. assists the sergeant in the accomplishment of police objectives in the area of human relations
   B. delegates responsibility to the sergeant in this critical area of administration so that he has freedom to develop a more wholesome program
   C. initiates the programs and policies which reflect the general views of the chief
   D. should direct but not participate in a human relations program

Questions 7-9.

DIRECTIONS: Questions 7 through 9 are to be answered SOLELY on the basis of the following paragraph.

   The sentiment of the community is not always favorable to procedures designed to accomplish the police purpose. Unfavorable public attitudes may make the immediate adoption of a superior procedure impractical. A necessary part of the task of achieving police objectives is the development of public attitudes favorable to their attainment. The police, therefore, must be organized to inform the public regarding the significance and consequences of failures in law enforcement and compliance, and also regarding police requirements and the results of failure to meet them. The police cannot progress ahead of public sentiment since there must be general acceptance by the people of controls that are applied by the police in order to completely accomplish the basic police objectives. The development of favorable public sentiment is a relatively long-range project, whereas organization requirements are immediate. The organizational structure, therefore, must be designed to conform somewhat to public attitudes. As public sentiment changes, modification of the structure may be desirable.

7. According to the above paragraph, modifications of the police organizational structure should 7.____
   A. be considered in instances where public sentiment has also changed
   B. be designed to anticipate major changes in public attitudes
   C. be regarded as a relatively long-range project
   D. follow closely any changes in public sentiment

8. According to the above paragraph, the development of favorable public attitudes towards the police is important because 8.____
   A. failures in law enforcement activity are thereby more likely to be quickly corrected
   B. the accomplishment of primary police purposes is largely dependent on such favorable attitudes
   C. the improvement of the conditions of work of the police are ultimately determined by the public
   D. no one will comply with police regulations without a favorable public attitude

9. According to the above paragraph, it would be MOST advisable that a decision to adopt a new police procedure 9.____
   A. be determined mainly by its crime deterring effect on the community
   B. not be made if any community objection has been expressed towards the procedure

C. be made only after favorable public attitudes have been developed in all community groups
D. be partly based on a consideration of its community acceptance

Questions 10-12.

DIRECTIONS: Questions 10 through 12 are to be answered SOLELY on the basis of the following paragraph.

All members of the police force must recognize that the people, through their representatives, hire and pay the police and that, as in any other employment, there must exist a proper employer-employee relationship. The police officer must understand that the essence of a correct police attitude is a willingness to serve, but at the same time he should distinguish between service and servility, and between courtesy and softness. He must be firm but also courteous, avoiding even an appearance of rudeness. He should develop a position that is friendly and unbiased, pleasant and sympathetic, in his relations with the general public, but firm and impersonal on occasions calling for regulation and control. A police officer should understand that his primary purpose is to prevent violations, not to arrest people. He should recognize the line of demarcation between a police function and passing judgment which is a court function. On the other side, a public that cooperates with the police, that supports them in their efforts and that observes laws and regulations may be said to have a desirable attitude.

10. In accordance with this paragraph, the PROPER attitude for a police officer to take is to

    A. be pleasant and sympathetic at all times
    B. be friendly, firm, and impartial
    C. be stern and severe in meting out justice to all
    D. avoid being rude, except in those cases where the public is uncooperative

11. Assume that an officer is assigned by his superior officer to a busy traffic intersection and is warned to be on the lookout for motorists who skip the light or who are speeding. According to this paragraph, it would be PROPER for the officer in this assignment to

    A. give a summons to every motorist whose car was crossing when the light changed
    B. hide behind a truck and wait for drivers who violate traffic laws
    C. select at random motorists who seem to be impatient and lecture them sternly on traffic safety
    D. stand on post in order to deter violations and give offenders a summons or a warning as required

12. According to this paragraph, a police officer must realize that the PRIMARY purpose of police work is to

    A. provide proper police service in a courteous manner
    B. decide whether those who violate the law should be punished
    C. arrest those who violate laws
    D. establish a proper employer-employee relationship

Questions 13-15.

DIRECTIONS: Questions 13 through 15 are to be answered SOLELY on the basis of the following paragraphs.

In cases of accident, it is most important for an officer to obtain the name, age, residence, occupation, and a full description of the person injured, names and addresses of witnesses. He shall also obtain a statement of the attendant circumstances. He shall carefully note contributory conditions, if any, such as broken pavement, excavation, lights not burning, snow and ice on the roadway, etc. He shall enter all the facts in his memorandum book and on Form 17 or Form 18, and promptly transmit the original of the form to his superior officer and the duplicate to headquarters.

An officer shall render reasonable assistance to sick or injured persons. If the circumstances appear to require the services of a physician, he shall summon a physician by telephoning the superior officer on duty and notifying him of the apparent nature of the illness or accident and the location where the physician will be required. He may summon other officers to assist if circumstances warrant.

In case of an accident or where a person is sick on city property, an officer shall obtain the information necessary to fill out card Form 18 and record this in his memorandum book and promptly telephone the facts to his superior officer. He shall deliver the original card at the expiration of his tour to his superior officer and transmit the duplicate to headquarters.

13. According to this passage, the MOST important consideration in any report on a case of accident or injury is to   13._____

    A. obtain all the facts
    B. telephone his superior officer at once
    C. obtain a statement of the attendant circumstances
    D. determine ownership of the property on which the accident occurred

14. According to this passage, in the case of an accident on city property, the officer should ALWAYS   14._____

    A. summon a physician before filling out any forms or making any entries in his memorandum book
    B. give his superior officer on duty a prompt report by telephone
    C. immediately bring the original of Form 18 to his superior officer on duty
    D. call at least one other officer to the scene to witness conditions

15. If the procedures stated in this passage were followed for all accidents in the city, an impartial survey of accidents occurring during any period of time in this city may be MOST easily made by   15._____

    A. asking a typical officer to show you his memorandum book
    B. having a superior officer investigate whether contributory conditions mentioned by witnesses actually exist
    C. checking all the records of all superior officers
    D. checking the duplicate card files at headquarters

Questions 16-18.

DIRECTIONS: Questions 16 through 18 are to be answered SOLELY on the basis of the following paragraph.

When the frequency of special situations that create extraordinary needs for police service is nearly continuous, as is often the case in a large city, a separate unit for each is desirable even though in some communities these needs are met by the force assigned to deal with the average need. Variations in the manpower needed to deal with special situations further complicate the problem. Special squads created to meet unusual needs are not likely to be adequate to deal with all situations. One unit must be used to supplement the other in some situations. Likewise, the force normally used to meet the average need must be used in some other situations to supplement the efforts of both. For example, the entire force is likely to be pressed into overtime duty when disaster strikes. The existence of special units, however, diminishes the frequency and extent of necessary requisitions of unspecialized manpower from their regular assignments. The special squads should also be used as a manpower reserve to fill vacancies in or absences from regular assignments when the regular services must be maintained exactly as before.

16. The one of the following situations which would MOST justify the creation of a separate unit, according to the above passage, is when

   A. the force assigned to deal with the average need, in small or large cities, is assigned continuously to handle all extraordinary needs for police service
   B. the frequency of the situations that create above average needs is somewhat in proportion to the size of the city
   C. the force assigned to deal with the average need has to give nearly continuous attention to above-average needs
   D. in a large city the separate unit can be used to supplement the force assigned to deal with the average need

17. When a special squad is unable to meet adequately one of the needs for police service which it was assigned to provide, it would be MOST correct, according to the above passage, to state that

   A. the force normally used to meet the average need should not be used unless some other special squad has first been assigned
   B. the force normally used to meet the average need as well as any other special squad should not both be used at the same time
   C. some other special unit should be used to supplement the special squad while attempting to avoid assigning the force normally used to meet the average need
   D. some other special unit should not be used unless it is likely that its own efforts can be supplemented by the special squad at some future time

18. The decision as to whether officers assigned to a special unit should be used to replace absent officers in a regular unit depends MAINLY on the

   A. extent to which unspecialized manpower must be requisitioned
   B. effect of the absences on the regular services which should not be even temporarily diminished

C. extent to which the services provided by the force normally assigned to the regular unit have been diminished by the absences
D. relative importance of maintaining the services of the special squad exactly as before

Questions 19-20.

DIRECTIONS: Questions 19 through 20 are to be answered SOLELY on the basis of the following paragraph.

The traditional characteristics of a police organization, which do not foster group-centered leadership, are being changed daily by progressive police administrators. These characteristics are authoritarian and result in a leader-centered style with all deter- mination of policy and procedure made by the leader. In the group-centered style, policies and procedures are a matter for group discussion and decision. The supposedly modern view is that the group-centered style is the most conducive to improving organizational effectiveness. By contrast, the traditional view regards the group-centered style as an idealistic notion of psychologists. It is questionable, however, that the situation determines the appropriate leadership style. In some circumstances, it will be leader-centered; in others, group-centered. Nevertheless, police supervisors will see more situations calling for a leadership style that, while flexible, is primarily group-centered. Thus, the supervisor in a police department must have a capacity not just to issue orders, but to engage in behavior involving organizational leadership which primarily emphasizes goals and work facilitation.

19. According to the above passage, there is reason to believe that with regard to the effectiveness of different types of leadership, the

    A. leader-centered type is better than the individual-centered type or the group-centered type
    B. leader-centered type is best in some situations and the group-centered type best in other situations
    C. group-centered type is better than the leader-centered type in all situations
    D. authoritarian type is least effective in democratic countries

20. According to the above passage, police administrators today are

    A. more likely than in the past to favor making decisions on the basis of discussions with subordinates
    B. likely in general to favor traditional patterns of leadership in their organizations
    C. more likely to be progressive than conservative
    D. practical and individualistic rather than idealistic in their approach to police problems

KEY (CORRECT ANSWERS)

1. D
2. B
3. B
4. D
5. D

6. A
7. A
8. B
9. D
10. B

11. D
12. A
13. A
14. B
15. D

16. C
17. C
18. B
19. B
20. A

POLICE SCIENCE NOTES
POLICE-COMMUNITY RELATIONS

A few years ago, the terminology used in describing the communication effort or system operating between the police and the community was "Police Public Relations," but today the appropriate words are "Police-Community Relations" (PCR). The single word change indicates an extremely different viewpoint as to what the appropriate communications should be between the police and the public they serve. In fact, even the hyphen between the words "police" and "community" is heavy with meaning.

PCR is a crime fighting, law enforcement concept in which the police and their community members, the citizens of the areas in which the police agency operates, involves themselves in communicating their objectives and problems to each other. Each group benefit from the wholesome exchange of viewpoints, and the objective toward which both move is a cooperative effort in which the police provide enforcement for and to the community according to professional and public requirements and the public assists in this effort. It is a human relations effort by both parties.

PCR is based on the human relations concept. Human relations is the whole area of study and practice aimed at establishing cooperative rather than antagonistic relationships between persons or groups. Human relations is based on effective communication so that with full and accurate knowledge of the situations all parties face, and based on realistic and rational methods of operation, all parties involved will benefit through an exchange relationship rather than one which is exploitive or superior-subordinate.

PCR involves the police department as an organization and its relationships with various segments of the community, and each member of the department and his relationships are developed through his individual contacts as a peace officer. The image conveyed by the individual officer conveys an image of the department as a whole; the image of the police agency becomes part of that which is seen by persons who individually contact each officer.

There have been at least three important changes in the relationships between the police and the community in recent years. The first is that police contacts are no longer nearly exclusively with professional criminals. The advent of the motor car and its development into the agency by which most people transport themselves has caused the police to come into contact with persons from all walks of life. This increased contact has given the police increased realization that the need for support from the law-abiding citizens of the community is imperative, which backing is soon lost when contacts by unprofessional officers are too frequent.

The second change is that to service oriented police operations which are demanded by the community and provided by the police. In some areas the police agency has become the governmental unit through which many and varied requests for services from government and private groups are channelled for reference to the appropriate organization which will provide the desired assistance.

The change is that of the role of the professional police as arbitrators of competing demands by special interest groups or individuals in the society. The job of the police remains repressive in many instances, but this must be performed in a society which is basically permissive and expressive—freedom of dissent is an extremely important right in a democratic society such as ours. It must be protected, and the police are often the only agency which is immediately available to offer such a service.

PCR aims toward community involvement with the police in their efforts to provide effective law enforcement. Although it would be more pleasant if more persons within the society were to like the police, and this can be accomplished to a certain extent by an effective PCR program, the more important objective of a PCR program is to convince the various individuals and groups in the society to work with the police. It may be necessary to obtain compliance by force and repression in some instances, but it is much to be preferred to win the willing compliance of persons and groups and their assistance in repression of unlawful behavior.

Democracy can function only when the rule of law is deemed by the majority to be the appropriate procedure to follow in obtaining protection and domestic tranquility. Democracy cannot function where anarchy and violence prevail to the point at which the system of designated, governmental, community controls become ineffective.

Officer must not neglect the fact that PCR programs involve the willingness and necessity to beliefs held in the community. PCR is not a one-way street as was the public relations system. PCR programs and their objectives include at least the following:

Information exchange forums, meetings, and programs by which the police and various community groups and their representatives (some of whom will display very antagonistic feelings toward the police and the lawfully constituted government) communicate their objectives and beliefs.

Communications systems through which the police and minority groups involve themselves with mutual solutions to problems facing each other.

Programs designed to: inform the public of crime problems facing the police; provide information to the community which will enable them to protect themselves from being victims of criminals; and promote the inflow of information to the police which will enable them to more effectively repress criminal activity.

Enlightening sessions designed to educate individual officers so that they will become aware of the fact (and believe in the efficacy of the basic construction of our social system) that he as an officer is working for the community and should not act as a free agent in interpreting laws or forcing citizens to conform to rules of conduct which have not been formalized by officially recognized governmental action.

PERSONAL CONDUCT

The individual actions taken or motivations and beliefs shown by an officer during his contacts with the public reflect upon the competence of the whole police department. Word of unprofessional conduct by individual officers spreads quickly like the waves of the sea and affect the responses of nearly unbelievable numbers of others in short order. These suggestions should be carefully considered and followed by all officers:

1. The professional officer is courteous, sincere, and friendly even when those whom he is contacting are abrasive, demanding, or insincere.

2. The professional officer is able to be at ease with all types of persons and communicate and interact with them with consideration, tact, and poise.

3. The professional officer shows respect to not only his superiors but also to his coworkers and subordinates.

4. The professional officer's person, uniform, and equipment are always clean, presentable and/or in good condition and repair.

5. The professional officer is always willing to provide any reasonable service to those in need.

6. The professional officer's conduct is exemplary whether he is on duty or not.

Our law enforcement system is based on the premise that every peace officer is also a citizen—a member of the community who is serving the community needs rather than operating to attain his own personal objectives exclusively. The role is a sacred one and must be upheld by each and every member of the police profession.

PUBLIC RELATIONS
CONTENTS

1. Public Relations and Its Tools 1
2. Image 1
3. The Public; Public Support 1
4. Responsibility 1
5. Supervision 1-2
6. Policy and Procedures 2
7. News Responsibility at Headquarters 2
8. Spot News 2-3
9. Suggested Criminal Case News Guide Lines 3
10. Pre-Arrest 3
11. News on Arrest 3-4
12. Post-Arrest Statements 4
13. News Other than Cases and Investigations 4-5
14. Day-to-Day Contacts with the Public 5
15. Public Relations Devices 5
16. Complaints Against Officers 5-6
17. Correspondence 6
18. Speeches and Public Appearances 6
19. Personal Contacts 6

PUBLIC RELATIONS

1. PUBLIC RELATIONS AND ITS TOOLS-Public Relations is developing public understanding of and respect for an organization and the work of the organization. The two basic tools for doing this are: (1) the news media, including newspapers, radio, television and magazines and (2) individual contacts of members of the public with the organization"s facilities and personnel.

   Trying to provide a superior service is not enough. For good public relations, every law enforcement agency must have, in addition, a properly outlined, carefully supervised, and frequently evaluated public relations program. The program should have a place in the training and duty assignments of every officer.

   Law enforcement must always face the fact that numbers of citizens have what seem to the citizen sufficient reasons to be annoyed with or resentful of the officer, either because of his dealings with them or because of some fancied failure in his dealings with others. Law enforcement officers are engaged in the business of making citizens conform to the law. This is bound to irk large numbers of citizens.

   The officer and his organization cannot rely on the public to be kind and not too critical and the officer must make every effort to develop and continue a public relations program to offset adverse public reactions.

2. IMAGE.-Public understanding of and respect for an organization is referred to as its "image." It is not necessary that any law enforcement organization (or officer) have a lovable public image. It is essential, however, to have an image respected by the public. It is also essential that the public have full awareness of the fact that the law enforcement agency and its officers are not engaged in a pleasant game of "catch-me-if-you-can" but are in the business of protecting life, limb and property against destruction or loss. And that this includes a killing or maiming by a drunk or careless vehicle operator, a strangling by a rapist or a homicide by a robber, or any other offense.

3. THE PUBLIC; PUBLIC SUPPORT.-Good public relations get good public support and the effectiveness of any public agency is dependent in large measure on public support. Good public relations for police should begin with a real concern for proper development of the attitude of the public towards the police agency itself and towards law enforcement. The proper public attitude to be sought is not just one favorable to the law enforcement agency but is also one of opposition to law-breaking, of demand for apprehension and punishment of violators generally, and of voluntary compliance by the general public with all laws and ordinances.

   A good public relations program should also inform the public as to the agency's organization, history, facilities, functions, objectives, progress, and what return the public is getting on its law-enforcement dollar.

   All factual information which can be disseminated concerning the work that the agency is doing and the investigations and arrests it is handling should be promptly given out.

4. RESPONSIBILITY.-Law enforcement agencies exercise powers of interrogation and of arrest. They, therefore, have a moral responsibility to keep the public as well informed as possible concerning activities in making arrests and taking people into custody.

5. SUPERVISION.-Public relations must be a matter of major concern for the Chief, Sheriff, or commanding officer of every law enforcement agency. He must give proper initiative to planning, establish definite rules for public relations and news releases and provide training

for personnel in public relations matters. He must make specific assignment of areas of responsibility, down to and including the be9at or patrol officer.

6. POLICY AND PROCEDURES.—Established procedures must exist for ensuring that newsworthy items are immediately brought to the attention of a responsible officer, so that he can take necessary action, including obtaining necessary added detail and locating news media representatives.

    Where one news representative has been furnished information on a story, all other news representatives in the pertinent areas should be furnished the same information when they call in or otherwise check with the law enforcement agency. Only in rare circumstances would it be appropriate for the law enforcement agency to assume the burden of contacting all news media.

    A continuing policy of fair and equal treatment for all news-media representatives is a basic requirement. However, when an individual reporter or television or other newsman initiates, on his own, a story which falls outside the spot-news category (such as an inside look at the operations of the department) or develops his own independent story, good relations with news media would dictate a respect for his work and cooperation in that specific instance on an exclusive basis.

    A law enforcement agency must train its officers to understand that the agency properly deals only in facts. It is the job of the news media to make the "story."

    In preparing rules for releasing news, it is necessary to consider times when parts of the news must be withheld for reasons of law (such as details on a crash of a military aircraft carrying classified equipment) or for reasons of decency (such as notifying next of kin of a death in an automobile accident before releasing the identity of the deceased to the press).

    As a basic rule, if the next of kin in death cases cannot be notified within a reasonable time, the reason should be determined and the news media then advised of the accident and the victims. The fact that a victim has not been identified or that next of kin has not been notified does not require withholding the fact that a fatal accident has occurred. Generally, in fatal accidents, a two-hour period of delay on the identity of the victim or victims, to give time to notify next-of-kin of the death or deaths, is an acceptable rule. After the two hours has passed, the news media may be informed of the identities but should also be informed that the next of kin have not yet been notified, when the law enforcement agency has been unable to give notice to the next-of-kin.

7. NEWS RESPONSIBILITY AT HEADQUARTERS.—Where news media contact a law enforcement installation for news, there should be clearly fixed responsibility for handling such calls, whether made in person or on the telephone.

    An officer should be assigned and responsible. He must be informed at all times on all matters which might be news.

    Officers so assigned must be trained to know departmental policy and special circumstances which would relate to the dissemination of each news item. The law enforcement agency should develop and put into effect policy which would make it unnecessary for the officer assigned news contacts to "check" with anyone on news stories, or otherwise make a cumbersome project of a story. The responsible officer should have a real desire to give out as much news as possible.

8. SPOT NEWS.—Where news media representatives are at the scene, factual information should be promptly provided by the law enforcement officer in charge. He can provide the

most accurate factual summary. He must carefully avoid guessing, making estimates, or furnishing conclusions.

If an officer is alone, he should follow the same rule of furnishing only factual information, without drawing conclusions, giving "an educated guess" or otherwise departing from exact fact.

Officers must bear in mind that they are almost never the sole source to whom news media can turn for information.

Officers on the scene should deal frankly and fairly with the representatives of the press, radio, and TV. Let the newsmen be the judges of what is news. Officers must exercise judgment to ensure that information furnished is factual and will not hinder official duties or damage the case.

9. SUGGESTED CRMINAL CASE NEWS GUIDE LINES.-The following guide lines are suggested as of value in planning and considering news matters in criminal cases. They will protect against improprieties and statements which may prejudice cases in court. They will permit cooperation with news media in areas of legitimate news interest and permit them to fulfill their responsibility to the public. They will insure that law enforcement fulfills its duty to keep its actions public and not secret, where this is proper.

10. PRE-ARREST.-When a crime occurs, news media may be furnished all pertinent facts relating to the crime itself. Items of evidence, which, if disclosed, would be prejudicial to the solution of the case, should not be made public.

    Photographs of a person accused by indictment or warrant, without any police identification material on the photographs, may be furnished.

    Where the identity of a suspect has not been established, it may be desirable to publicize descriptions, artists' sketches or other information which could lead to the identification and arrest of the suspect.

    Suspects who are interviewed but not charged should not be identified.

    The finding of physical evidence such as weapons or proceeds of the crime, the issuance and service of a search warrant and the positive or negative results of the search, may be released. Information as to how a weapon or proceeds of the crime were located should be withheld, if it involves data which are prejudicial.

    Fugitive cases may require wide publicity. However, in some fugitive cases it may be necessary to withhold information when its publication would be harmful to the apprehension of the wanted person. Common sense should dictate the manner in which fugitive cases are handled, with a positive view toward the public interest and safety and the protection of other law enforcement agencies in the case of possibly dangerous, armed, psychotic and similar fugitives.

    Fugitives who have a history of being armed, or a propensity for violent acts, should be characterized as dangerous, so that an arresting officer will be well aware of any dangerous aspects involved in an apprehension of the fugitive.

11. NEWS ON ARREST.-Personnel authorized to deal with news media should supply any relevant information on an arrest, provided it could not be later construed as prejudicial to a fair trial. Information which may properly be given out includes:
    (1) Defendant's name, age, residence, employment, marital status and similar back ground information.

(2) Substance or text of charge on which the arrest was made (and the identity of the person preferring the charge, if such information will not cause danger or embarrassment to the complainant).
    a. Identification of persons preferring charges should always be withheld when the person is a victim of a sex crime and publication of the identity would be a matter of serious embarrassment to the victim.
(3) Identify of the investigating and arresting agency, police personnel involved, duration of the investigation and aspects of the investigation of a non-prejudicial nature.
(4) Circumstances surrounding arrest, including time and place, resistance (if any), pursuit, possession and use of weapons and a description of items seized at the time of arrest.
(5) Photographs of a defendant, without police identification data in them, may be furnished to news media. Officers should not assist in posing prisoners for news or television cameramen, nor hinder their efforts in taking pictures during the course of any normal movement of prisoners which expose them to public view.
(6) Where there is any question in an officer's mind as to whether an item should be released, he should follow the general principle that information should be made available unless it could reasonably be construed as prejudicial to the prisoner or harmful to a later prosecution or defense of the prisoner.

12 POST-ARREST STATEMENTS-To avoid the possibility of jeopardizing prosecution of a criminal matter by prejudicing the right of a defendant to a fair trial, statements should NOT be made to news media in the period between arrest and trial, relating to:
(1) Character or reputation of a suspect or the existence, if any, of a prior criminal record.
(2) Existence of a confession, admission or statement by an accused person, or the absence of such.
(3) Re-enactment of a crime or the fact that a defendant may have shown investigators where a weapon, loot or other evidence was located.
(4) References to a defendant as (for example) a "sex maniac," "depraved character," "typical gangster," "notorious criminal," etc.
(5) Examinations or tests which the defendant may have taken or have refused to take.
    a. Since the V & T Law gives the privilege of declining to take an alcohol test in Driving While Intoxicated or Driving While Ability Impaired cases, and embodies this in the crime or infraction, press inquiries as to taking such a test (but not its results) may be answered.
(6) Guilt or innocence of a defendant.
(7) Identity, credibility or testimony of prospective witnesses.
(8) Any information of a purely speculative nature.

13. NEWS OTHER THAN CASES AND INVESTIGATIONS.-A very considerable number of things connected with law enforcement other than cases and investigation are newsworthy. It takes training, attention, and a fixing of responsibility to ensure that the news in such items is recognized, developed, and made available to news media.

The responsible officer must be kept fully informed of plans and activities in all parts of his agency. He must have adequate authority to develop the added detail and facts which experience will teach him are necessary to a good story.

A discussion of this kind of news and a constant refresher on its value should regularly be on the agenda of every law enforcement agency's staff meetings and conferences of ranking officers. Newsmen will be good guides as to what is news and what detail will be required, but it will take constant attention and thought on the part of the law enforcement agency to recognize and pull out the things which may develop into usable stories.

14. DAY-TO-DAY CONTACTS WITH THE PUBLIC.-Good community relations require that the law enforcement agency and the individual officer be genuinely interested in people and their problems. The police officer is "on the scene" daily, while on patrol. He is the only public official most people of a community see or have contact with with any frequency. Disinterest of a law enforcement agency or officer in local problems, even when they are not essentially police problems, will be variously interpreted as police hostility, police slackness or police ineptitude. Disinterest is very bad public relations.

"Appearance" and "proper attitude" are key words for good public contacts. A poor appearance, lack of civility or other poor attitude can do more to engender poor public relations than an uncaught burglar. People expect that not all burglars will be caught. They do not expect that their law enforcement facilities or officers will have a poor appearance. They do expect that their officers will be entirely civil and interested in their complaints.

The appearance of facilities must be cared for by fixing responsibility for physical condition and maintenance and by inspections to ensure that such responsibility is carried out. The appearance of personnel and equipment must be cared for by adequate training, adequate rules, and adequate inspections.

Civility is an absolute requirement for any law enforcement officer, but an excess of courtesy is not required and may often be misunderstood.

Much of the public relations value from contacts with citizens depends on the officer's civility and his display of interest in the citizen and his problem.

An officer who gives close and civil attention to a complainant and handles the complaint in a mediocre way does a far better public relations job than the officer who is apparently indifferent to and bored with the citizen's problem, but who handles the problem promptly and superbly. Each officer should, of course, handle every problem to the best of his ability. But excellent handling will not overcome a poor personal contact with the citizen.

Sarcasm, flippancy, brusqueness, or being overbearing lose officers more respect than failure to solve a serious case.

15. PUBLIC RELATIONS DEVICES.-All law enforcement administrators should give thought to public relations devices, such as pamphlets to be issued by the law enforcement agency, sponsorship by the agency of youth activity, such as athletics or Christmas shows, exhibits to be prepared and shown at school and public events, and similar "self-starting" types of things. These are all useful and desirable. They require considerable initiative or "self-starting" on the part of the law enforcement agency and its top officials. For example, a pamphlet on parking facilities and techniques in a downtown area, with references to pertinent laws and ordinances, is obviously an undertaking requiring time, effort and "push," although it need not be costly. This type of public relations device is well worthwhile.

16. COMPLAINTS AGAINST OFFICERS.-Basic ingredients of a good public relations program include established regulations and procedures for handling complaints against officers. Complaints should be regarded as signals calling attention to possible misconduct, or dereliction of duty, or public misunderstanding or misconception, or, perhaps, to mere inefficiency.

The regulations must insure that every person complaining about an officer receives fair and civil treatment and is thoroughly interviewed and that a written report is made thereafter to the chief, sheriff, or commanding officer. In addition to being good

POLICE SCIENCE NOTES

BASIC CONCEPTS OF LAW AND ARREST

Man has been puzzling over the appropriateness of community controls throughout his recorded history and undoubtedly before that. What he has been trying to decide are the answers to: "Who is/are going to run the show?" "Under what restrictions must authority operate?" and "What acts by community members shall be required or prohibited?" Basic to an understanding of the complexity of answers to these questions is an awareness of the variety of systems and laws under which various societies have lived and are living. At some time some community has lived under laws directly opposite to those under which we now control ourselves, and their requirements were "right" for that time and place. In fact, we can bring to mind examples of changes which have occurred in our own United States of America during its existence—even within our own lifetime. The requirements placed upon the members of any community by its government consist of laws which filter out by prevailing over others in the market place of ideas and which are manifested by their issuance through formal governmental organizations.

Every police office should be aware of the fact that there is no law which has not been enacted in response to and for the purpose of correcting a problem which has become significant by the degree to which some member of the community have acted in opposition to the common belief. In short, where there is no meaningful opposition to the feelings of the majority there is no law in support of those beliefs. For example, cannibalism is not prohibited in the United States because opposition to it is so pervasive that it is reasonable to say that only the mentally ill have engaged in that gruesome activity.

Individuals and communities require guidelines defining acceptable conduct and reciprocal duties and responsibilities in order to attain feelings of tranquility, a sense of well-being, and a belief that conformance to group requirements will result in the society's respect for and supply of individual needs in response. Basic to any society, primitive or modern, is the necessity for disciplined behavior, and the necessity for community tranquility. Each individual must relinquish his right to act entirely for his own self-interest in return for the agreement of others not to deprive him unduly of his right to personal freedom or to impinge upon his reciprocal rights under the law. Every requirement of law acts to some degree to reduce individual freedom of action, but reasonable restrictions on absolute freedom are essential to community living and to protect individuals against others. As the danger to any community belief increases so will the group response grow in severity to reduce that threat, especially when the common belief is basic and widely accepted without reservation.

Police officers are faced with daily frustration caused by their inability to understand clearly that the freedom-loving citizens of our Nation have learned from past experience (some of which initiated our Nation's birth) that absolute authority demands rigid compliance with even the smallest and relatively unimportant requirement and results in stultifying repression of personal freedom. The ultimately efficient government can only be one in which power is so centralized that it is dictatorial and undemocratic. Therefore, laws have developed which restrict the police to that level of efficiency which is acceptable to the citizens and which permits the greatest possible individual freedom. Again, there is no law where there is no problem. Therefore, there should be little serious doubt that one of the highest duties of a police officer is to know and follow the law because it has been developed in answer to previously existing actions which were conducted in opposition to the beliefs of the people. Officials who are responsible for law enforcement must personify lawfulness as they interact with offenders. A peace officer is endowed with awesome power over life and property, and he must not only restrict his actions to those the law but also restrain himself personally to be considered a thoughtful, objective, police professional.

It is important that every police officer understands the basics of the checks and balances system under which we govern ourselves. Our forefathers so constructed our governmental system that none of the three branches of our government—the legislature, the executive, and the judicial—could become so strong that it would be able to dominate the people completely. The basic objective of this system is to prevent one or a few people from absolute control and overwhelming power. In its operation, the checks and balances system prevents domination by providing stumbling blocks in the paths of requirements which do not meet with the approval of the great majority of the citizens. Without considerable support, legislatures will not pass laws, the executive branch will not actively enforce them, and the courts will overturn them. However, those requirements which are backed by the great majority of the people are enacted by legislatures, enforced with great universality and vigor by the executive branch, and upheld by the courts.

The individual professional police officer understands the checks and balances system and acts within the law because of this knowledge. At the operational level, even though a patrol officer is aware of a problem he does not attempt to "enforce the law" when the legislature has not passed a statute dealing with it. He neither strains to fit the facts of an incident into another statute nor makes an arrest for an unrelated offense in order to harrass the "law breaker." At the executive level, the professional police administrator or agency head allocates the resources of his department according to priorities so that enforcement of important offenses is emphasized. The accompanying spinoff is naturally the de-emphasis of enforcement against those offenses which are determined to be of lesser importance. The term which applies to this assignment of priorities is *selective enforcement*.

Professional Demeanor

The appropriateness of the reasons for and the manner by which members of a community are deprived of their liberty is one of the most difficult problems to be solved by members of a society and its lawmakers. An arrest or detention is a matter of preventing the free movement of a person. In most cases, what is more important to the person subject to this deprivation of liberty is the manner in which an arrest or detention is effected. There is a great difference between simply following the directions of another without the free will to do any other thing one might wish to do and that loss *plus* being searched, handcuffed, placed in obvious incarceration, and even being stripped of all clothing and dignity for the purpose of maximizing security. In fact, most people will understand the necessity of appropriate loss of liberty, but what makes them seriously upset is the public spectacle and loss of face which it can entail when improperly conducted, especially when the arresting officer shows personal antagonism toward the prisoner.

The professional officer balances the importance of each factor involved in an arrest situation. Although safety to himself, his fellow officers and the general public is very important, he is well aware that it is not always the most important factor. In fact, he knows that some persons will submit to an arrest quietly unless demeaning security precautions are utilized or personal antagonism is manifested by the arresting officer. Unfortunately, the unprofessional officer often considers security and safety to be uppermost and controlling in nearly every case and is personally offended by lawbreakers. When these conditions prevail, arrested and detained persons are often subjected to such overwhelming threats to their psychological well-being (or face) that they find it necessary to fight back against those who are creating the threat. In some cases their loss of face or distress is so great that they physically attack any person who obstructs their liberty and are willing to kill to escape rather than to suffer the public humiliation of detention or arrest. Therefore, the professional officer effects his detentions and arrests with circumspection and avoids excessive psychological distress to those being restricted. By making the arrest as easy as possible on the offender, the arresting officer also makes it as easy as possible on himself and his coworkers. The professional exerts his will over those whom he is arresting by the use of reasoning rather than his club. The officer who is involved in fights significantly more often than his coworkers, however soon becomes well known and is avoided as a partner.

Persons usually react in three general ways to a police officer who is enforcing the law or is about to make an arrest. They may submit to his directions or the arrest without resistance. Such persons follow the directions of the officer because they believe that the officer is correct in what he is doing or they simply bow to the inevitable. The professional, skilled police officer will so conduct himself that the great majority of persons will react to his directions in this way.

Other persons may feel gravely threatened by the officer's actions and believe it necessary to attack either verbally or physically, or flee. Whatever their action may be, it is an attempt to reduce the real or imagined threat to their physical or mental well-being. Although the attack will usually be directed at the source of the threat, the officer, it may be against another person—an "innocent" third party. This is still an attempt to reduce their feelings of frustration, however, but the target will be an object or person who cannot "fight back." We have all witnessed examples of distressed persons who kick their cats, shout at their children, or drive their automobiles recklessly when frustrated. In fact, many times officers find themselves to be the "cat" whom it is necessary for the person to "kick" to compensate for a frustrating experience which occurred prior to the officer's arrival on the scene. The professional officer, because of his self-confidence, is never threatened by verbal "cat kicking." He is able to control these excited persons through the use of his calm, professional, competent manner so that they soon begin to accept his directions. This same technique is usually effective with those offenders who are inclined towards physical attack. The experienced professional officer knows with reasonable accuracy those who cannot be dissuaded and with reasonable force acts to protect himself and others from physical attack.

The professional officer asks himself questions such as these: "This person is attacking me verbally, therefore, he (NOT I) is greatly threatened by something. Am I the threat, or is it something else?" "Is this attack going to be all talk, or will it turn into a physical attack?" "What can I do to reduce his feeling of distress?" The unprofessional reacts out of his own fear of the verbal attack, retaliates in kind, and the situation rapidly escalates into physical combat or the bringing of inappropriate charges out of spite. Invariably the result of retaliatory action by an officer who attacks to save his own face, no matter how poorly the offender may have acted to initiate the incident, is the salvation of the offender's conscience. This is because the offender will be able to say to himself that the officer attacked him, therefore, no matter what the offender has done, the officer has become the "bad guy" who is subject to all the blame—the "offensive cat," if you will

The third reaction is that of ignoring or remaining unaffected by the threat. Persons who manifest this type of reaction are those who are secure, unconcerned, and believe that they are truly not endangered by the threat. They are convinced that those who are acting aggressively towards them cannot in fact harm them in any basic way. In everyday language, this type of individual is called a person with "self-confidence." It is this type of confidence that the professional police officer exhibits. It is a quiet confidence, as opposed to the blatant, pushy, aggressive, officious manner of those who are unsure of themselves and who try to make up for it with bluster, which is immediately recognizable as a lack of confidence.

Self-confidence is the kind of attitude which makes it possible to exert one's will upon others while encountering the least resistance from them. The officer who exhibits this confidence brings the belief into the minds of those he is controlling that: "This officer will not ask anything of me which is not only lawful but also reasonable and necessary, and if I refuse to act in response to his requests, I will be not only lawful but also unreasonable and appear foolish to others." On the other hand, if it is the person who is to be arrested who exhibits the self-confidence, that person is the one who has the greatest chance of defeating the officer and taking over control of the situation. The officer who allows himself to be manipulated is in for a very uncomfortable experience. The danger to the officer is rarely that of physical attack, rather he will feel greatly threatened psychologically. He may begin to believe that he is appearing foolish and damaged in his self-image (loss of face; receiving severe blows to his ego, etc.). Unless he retains his self-control, he may well commit a rash or illegal act which can easily result in disciplinary action or a civil suit naming him and his department as defendants. But the experienced professional officer never loses during these encounters because: He never presses or demands more than is absolutely necessary; Even though the law may empower him to do more; He always acts within the law and utilized it to accomplish its basic purpose, not just technical requirements which were designed to accomplish some other objective. His actions assure that his opponent becomes aware that: What the officer requires is within the law; The full extent of the available powers are never utilized without full reason; The officer never acts out of personal vengeance.

Professional Direction

ONLY ROOKIES TRY TO ENFORCE ALL THE LAWS ALL THE TIME, AND ONLY ROOKIES CONFINE THEIR ENFORCEMENT ACTIVITY ALMOST EXCLUSIVELY TO AN ARREST. The experienced professional officer has learned that enforcement of some laws is best accomplished by simply being present and visible. Other laws can be enforced by a warning or an educationally oriented conversion with actual or potential offenders. There are certain laws which do require that offenders be processed through the criminal justice system by either a summons or physical arrest. In most jurisdictions, with rare exceptions, no officer is in fact required to arrest for an offense except when ordered to do so by a magistrate, either by the judge in person or under his written order in the form of a warrant.

Criminal Law

A crime or an offense is an act or omission forbidden by law, prosecuted by the governmental officials of the jurisdiction, and punishable upon conviction. The statutes which define what acts or omissions are crimes or offenses must clearly state the kind of conduct which is prohibited or required and designate the punishment which is to be applied to those adjudged guilty.

Each statute which defines a crime is constructed of elements or criteria which the prosecution must prove before a defendant may be found guilty of the charge. The words used in statutes each have very special and particular meaning under law, and an officer must be careful to be aware of these legal terms because definitions in law sometimes differ from the meanings they convey when used in informal or daily conversation. For example, larceny or theft involves the *taking of the personal property of another*. Each of the underlined words is an element of the offense, and they are not the only elements. The "thief has not taken if he has not gained possession, it is not personal property if it is an attachment to a house, and it is not another's if the thief is a part owner or the property has been abandoned. Furthermore, even f he does commit all those acts, he has not committed theft unless he intended to steal. For example, the acts were committed under his reasonable belief that the property was his. Also, no matter how fervent was his intention to steal, there cannot be a conviction where the item "stolen" was not subject to ownership which is protected by law, for example an illegal lottery ticket.

Detentions

Police officers are empowered to make detentions and arrests under appropriate restrictions. A detention is a temporary restriction of one's liberty during which the detaining person is permitted to make a short investigation for the purpose of determining whether or not the person detained is subject to arrest for an offense. The authority and restrictions upon it which apply to this power of an officer are delineated by either court decisions or statutes, dependent upon the law which prevails within a particular jurisdiction. This type of detention is generally referred to as "stop and frisk." These three little words, however, have become the subject of thousands of pages of court decisions and statutes. This manual must cover the subject with just a few words, and readers should bear in mind that jurisdictions differ in what is permissible. Each officer should become well versed in the law on this subject as it is applied in his jurisdiction.

The stop and detention of a person is generally authorized when an officer has reasonable grounds for suspecting that the individual whom he intends to detain: has committed a crime, is committing a crime, is about to commit a crime.

Note that the facts on which the officer bases his stop and detention are less than those necessary for him to effect an arrest, and it is essential to his authority that the person to be detained must be suspected of criminal activity. An arrest requires that the officer has reasonable grounds for *believing* that the person has committed or is committing a crime, but a detention requires the officer to have reasonable grounds for *suspecting* involvement in criminal activity. Because the officer is possessed of information short of that required to make an arrest, he may not use deadly force to stop or detain the person.

An important factor in the laws dealing with detentions is that of the duration which will be permitted. In jurisdictions where the courts have delineated the law on this subject, case law permits officers to detain persons a reasonable time. The duration permitted is determined by the relative importance of permitting the officer time necessary to ascertain whether or not the person has committed a crime and the loss of freedom suffered by the person detained. Each case is decided on its own facts. Where statutes control, legislatures either permit a reasonable time, similar to court holdings, or specifically limit the duration, varying from ten minutes to two hours. Under both case law and statutes, however, an officer in every jurisdiction is required to release the person immediately after he has determined that the person has not committed a crime. Where the duration is limited to a specified time period, when the time limit has expired, the officer must either arrest the person for a crime or immediately release him, even though with more time to investigate the officer might have been able to develop sufficient information to effect an arrest.

Another critical difference among the various jurisdictions is the right of the officer to transport the person detained during the course of the investigation. In some jurisdictions the officer is not permitted to remove the person from the place at which the detention was initiated. In areas where it is permitted, the transportation must be conducted only when it is reasonably necessary for the purpose of investigating the possible criminal involvement of the person detained, and unless the investigation results in the person's arrest he should be returned to the place from which he was removed. The officer may ask any pertinent question of the person detained, for example his name, an explanation of what he is doing or where he is going, the ownership of any property in his possession, etc., but the officer must constantly remain aware that the person detained is under no obligation to answer any question. The detained individual may remain absolutely silent during the whole period of detention, is under no obligation to produce any identification or other property for the officer's inspection, and the office has no right to take *anything* from the person except a weapon.

Frisks

The frisk is a very limited search which may be conducted by an officer who has detained a person. It may be performed only when the officer: knows that the person has a weapon in his immediate possession; reasonably suspects that the person has a weapon in his immediate possession.

Note that the frisk is for weapons only, and that the officer must be able to state the facts which caused the development of his belief that the person possessed a weapon. The frisk: must be only for the purpose of locating the weapon; must be initially restricted to touching or grasping only the *outer* clothing of the individual; may be continued inside the outer clothing, pockets, etc. only after the officer has felt something which reasonably causes him to believe that a weapon is contained within.

If the officer finds a weapon, he may remove it from the person's possession. If the possession of the weapon on the part of the person constitutes a crime, the officer may arrest for that offense and retain the weapon as evidence. If the person is not arrested, the officer shall return the weapon at the end of the detention.

Arrests

An arrest is the deprivation of one's liberty by another for the purpose of initiating the arrested person's processing through the justice system, usually the criminal justice system. An arrest must be made in compliance with the restrictions which surround such an action. Otherwise, it is considered a false arrest and will cause the loss of the admissibility of any resulting evidence and possible loss of a conviction. The arresting officer may also possibly be subject to a suit for civil damages and be charged with a crime. An "arrest" which is made without the intention for processing the party into or through the justice system would be kidnapping within the statutes of most jurisdictions. Arrests can be made either under the authority of an arrest warrant or without a warrant, and the arresting person can be either a police officer or a person.

An arrest involves the following elements:

1. The arresting party "intends" to take the arrested person into custody. Although in most cases the arresting party's actual intention is to take the person into custody, and the best way to express this is by stating words such as, "You are under arrest for...," courts determine the intention from all the defend himself from false arrest liability by simply claiming that he had no intention to arrest.

2. The arresting party acts under the belief that he has legal authority. If the arresting party is correct in his belief the arrest is valid, but if he actually does not have the authority, it is an illegal arrest. Examples of lack of authority would be arrests made under a void or non-existent warrant, even though the officer had been informed that there was a warrant, and arresting for a misdemeanor not committed in his presence, if this is not permitted in his jurisdiction.

3. The arresting party gains custody and control of the arrested person. An arrest is not complete until the arrested person comes within the custody and control of the arresting party, and this state exists when either the person submits or his resistance is overcome. It is not necessary that the person be touched or that any force be applied if he understands that he is in the power of the arresting person and submits to control; that his liberty is restrained is sufficient. On the other hand, if the officer's words, "You are under arrest for..." are immediately followed by the suspect's running away, there has been no arrest. In fact, unless the flight includes some physical contact or the application of force between the suspect and the arresting party, the flight does not constitute resisting arrest.

An arrest warrant is an order of a court directing police officers to arrest and bring before the court the person named in the warrant. If it is practicable, an officer should obtain a warrant before making an arrest. The basic purpose served by the warrant process is to protect persons from unjustified arrests and prosecutions. The warrant is one of the manifestations of the checks and balances system in that a member of the judicial branch passes upon the legitimacy of actions intended by the executive branch. Given the same circumstances or facts known to an officer, if he arrests after obtaining a warrant, the courts will in all probability sustain the arrest, but if he arrests without one his action will be much more closely scrutinized for probable cause.

Following are common requirements for a valid arrest warrant:

1. Probable Cause: The magistrate issuing the warrant must make an impartial judgment on the basis of the evidence presented that probable cause exists that a crime has been committed by the person to be arrested. Probable cause is more than mere suspicion on the part of the officer requesting the warrant, but he is not required to present proof beyond a reasonable doubt of the person's guilt. Information supplied by informants may be used, even if their identity is not disclosed, but officers must be able to state facts which indicate the probable reliability of such information which they have not acquired through their own observation.

2. Affidavit supported by oath or affirmation. Some person must swear to his belief in the truth of the statements contained in the affidavit.

3. Person Particularly Described: The description must be such that the officer serving the warrant is supplied with information sufficient for him to believe with reasonable certainty that the person whom he is about to arrest is the person described. Ordinarily the warrant includes the name of the person, but sometimes this is not known. In such cases, a physical description, occupation or place of employment, residence address or other information may be utilized to particularly describe the person.

4. Nature of the Offense: Although the language need not describe the offense with the same detail as in an indictment or information, it must be sufficient to inform the person of the subject of the accusation.

5. Officers Designated: The warrant may direct an individual officer or a class of officers to arrest the person. For example, the warrant may be addressed to all police officers in the state.

6. Issued in the Name of the Jurisdiction: Warrants must be issued either in the name of the state under which the issuing magistrate's authority exists or in the name of the United States when issued by a federal official.

7. Signed by the Issuing Official: Only an official authorized by law may sign a warrant, and he must be a neutral and impartial person, a magistrate, or judicial officer.

Requirements to Be Followed in Serving a Warrant:

1. Person serving warrant must be named in it. Either the officer or person serving the warrant must be specifically named in the warrant or he must be within the class of persons designated.

2. Must Be Served Within the Jurisdiction: A warrant issued in one state may not be served in another unless the second state has authorized this service by statute. An officer in the second state may arrest if he has knowledge of the warrant's issuance; however, his knowledge constituting the reasonable grounds for his belief that a felony has been committed by the person.

3. Officer Make Known His Purpose: Unless the information will imperil the arrest or the person flees or resists before the officer can convey his intention, the officer must inform the person of his intention to arrest and the cause of it.

4. Show the Warrant or Inform Person It Exists: Under common law, the officer must possess the warrant and show it to the person if he demands it, but most modern codes have relaxed this requirement under the needs of today's society. However, the officer's belief in the existence of the warrant must be reasonable, and it shall be shown to the person as soon as practicable if he so requests.

Arrests can be made without a warrant by both officers and private persons. The authority of a police officer is more extensive, but not as much so as most people believe.

1. Both an officer and a private person can arrest for a felony committed in their presence and for a felony which has actually been committed but not in their presence.

2. An officer can arrest for a felony which he reasonably believes has been committed by the individual to be arrested, even though the crime has not been committed, but a private person may not. Stated in another way, the officer is protected if he makes a reasonable mistake, but the private person is not.

3. In all jurisdictions an officer can arrest for a misdemeanor which is committed in his presence, but in some jurisdictions a private person may not.

4. In some jurisdictions an officer may arrest for a misdemeanor not committed in his presence when he has reasonable cause to believe that it has been committed by the suspect, but a private person may not do so in any jurisdiction.

The Constitution, statutes, and court decisions refer to the necessity of the "reasonable cause" and "probable cause" which must exist before the authority to arrest arises. This degree of proof, evidence, or information to be possessed by the officer who intends an arrest must be more than good faith suspicion (enough to effect a detention for investigation), but it need not be proof beyond a reasonable doubt of the person's guilt. The reasonable cause is determined as of the time the arrest is effected. Evidence acquired after the arrest may not be utilized to validate a preceding arrest. In fact, if the arrest is not based on probable cause that evidence will be excluded no matter how condemning and conclusive it might have been in proving the defendant's guilt.

The standards by which an officer's reasonable cause to arrest is ascertained is determined individually for each case. That is, the information in his possession and its relationship to the development of probable cause in his mind (as opposed to a reasonable man test) in the light of his personal experience and the circumstances of the case before the court will all be considered by the court in arriving at its holding that there was or was not probable cause to arrest. Actions which do not attract the attention of untrained or inexperienced persons or officers may convince the experienced and trained officer that a particular offense is being committed. This experience may include not only the activity but also the person performing it. An officer who knows of the past criminal record of a suspect may consider that history along with other facts in developing reasonable cause, but the officer may not arrest on only the basis of one's previous criminal record.

The following are sources which can develop reasonable cause to arrest for the officer:

1. Complaints From Victims and Information From Witnesses: Statements and information received which indicate that a crime has been committed and which provide evidence by which the offender can be ascertained by developing reasonable cause to arrest. An officer must bear in mind that if the crime complained of is less than a felony no arrest will be valid unless a warrant is first issued, unless their jurisdiction is one in which officers are permitted to arrest for misdemeanors on reasonable cause. But if the jurisdiction is one in which private persons can arrest for misdemeanors, the victim or a witness can make the arrest and turn the prisoner over to the officer.

2. Information From an Informant: The reliability of the informant is an important factor. An officer should maintain records on the cases in which the particular informant's information has proven to be accurate, and whenever possible the officer should make further investigation to determine that the information is correct prior to making his arrest without a warrant.

3. Observation of the Officer: When the officer witnesses the actual commission of the crime, there is reasonable grounds to arrest without serious question. But when his observations lead him to a reasonable suspicion only, then he must first detain until his investigation leads to reasonable cause to arrest. When all the circumstances lead the officer to the reasonable belief that a felony has been committed, he may arrest under his reasonable belief in any jurisdiction, but for a misdemeanor only if his jurisdiction permits that type of arrest. An officer can always obtain a warrant and effect the arrest later for the misdemeanor.

4. Physical Evidence: Fingerprints, identification dropped at the scene of the crime, footprints leading from the scene of the crime to the place of apprehension, and other physical evidence closely tying the suspect to the crime would be sufficient to give rise to reasonable cause to arrest.

5. Information Received from the Officer's Department or From Another Agency: Information received over the police radio, at briefings, or from wanted circulars or lists may

form the basis for reasonable cause; however, persons initiating these messages must have reasonable cause for doing so.

Citation/Summons Process

The processing of offenders into the justice system is ordinarily begun when he is contacted by the police. At this point the person may be "physically" arrested and taken to jail or other place of detention to await his appearance before the court. Very few defendants want to spend time in jail, and the purpose of such incarceration is only to assure the appearance of the defendant before the magistrate. Originally, under our criminal law, incarceration to await court appearance was the only process utilized no matter what the degree of the offense. Beginning with the widespread use of the automobile and the numerous offenses committed by motorists, spurred by the growth of more liberal feelings toward offenders by both the general community and persons involved in the administration of justice, and because of the great savings in time and money which the method causes, written notification to an offender of the charge to be made and the time and place to appear before a magistrate has now become prevalent. Commonly called "a ticket," the citation or summons process is now not only used universally for traffic code offenses but has expanded to include many other types as well such as theft, assault, battery, a variety of regulatory statutes, and other misdemeanor offenses. Whenever possible or permitted, an officer should use this process.

The "ticket" procedure can proceed in three ways: an arrest followed by release, a detention followed by release, or the delivery of a notice of charges to be filed to the person charged. Although definitions differ somewhat, the citation process is that which involves an arrest by an officer followed by the offender's signing on the citation that he promises to appear in court at the time indicated, at which time he is given a copy of the citation and released from arrest. The defendant's signature and promise is his "bail." Should he fail to appear, he commits an offense which is separate from that of the original charge. The offender may refuse to sign the citation, but if he chooses to exert this right the officer is required to incarcerate him.

In jurisdictions in which the summons process is utilized, the offender is detained (not arrested) for a period necessary for the officer to determine the defendant's identity and write the summons, a copy is given to the person (he is not required to take it, and he is then released from detention. The suspect is not required to sign the summons, he commits no offense if he does not appear, and upon his non-appearance the court simply issues a warrant of arrest for the charge made.

The notice process involves leaving a written notice to be discovered by the person to be charged or otherwise delivering such notice, for example by mail. The vast majority of cases in which this process is used involves parking offenses, but it can also be utilized for many other offenses. Whether the person receives the notice or not, the charge is filed before the court, and if the defendant does not appear as directed in the notice, an arrest warrant will be issued by the court. Each officer must be aware of the law concerning these processes in his area because in many jurisdictions numerous offenses have been required by statutes and departmental regulations to be so handled. Therefore, an officer who incarcerates a person who is entitled under law or departmental regulation to be offered a citation or summons will be subject to prosecution, civil suit, and/or disciplinary action.

POLICE SCIENCE NOTES

FORCE, SEARCH, AND SEIZURE

Use of Force

The right to use force against another varies according to the reasonable and apparent necessity that it be applied. The most important factors considered in the determination of how much force may be used by an officer are the following:

1. Is the force used or contemplated essential, or could the actor reasonably foresee that less force would be sufficient?
2. Does the crime to be prevented or the arrest to be attempted involve a felony or misdemeanor?
3. Does the act or crime to be prevented by force endanger property rights or human life and limb, and to what extent?
4. What are the responsibilities under law between the actor and what or whom he is attempting to protect with force?
5. Do departmental regulations restrict officers to less force than that permitted by statutes and court decisions?

When necessary, a police officer is permitted to use force in the performance of his duty to accomplish the following objectives:

1. To preserve the peace, prevent commission of offenses, or prevent suicide or self-inflicted injury.
2. To make *lawful* arrests and searches, to overcome resistance to such arrests and searches, and to prevent escapes from custody.
3. To defend himself or another against unlawful evidence to his person or property.
4. To interrupt an intrusion on or interference with the lawful possession of property.

Lawful force is an aggressive act committed by a police officer in the performance of his duty when it is necessary to accomplish any of the objectives listed above. Deadly force is that which under the prevailing circumstances is capable of or intended to cause death or great bodily injury. Although lawful, or necessary, force is the minimum amount sufficient to achieve a legitimate objective, this does not mean that an officer is permitted to escalate the force he uses without limit until the police objective is accomplished. For example, it would be illegal and immoral for an office to use deadly force to prevent a person from unlawfully interfering with or even destroying anothers personal property such as an automobile, even if under the circumstances, shooting the person would be the only way the destruction could be stopped.

Deadly force may be used to prevent a felony which threatens the life or safety of a person. However, when the felony does not involve such danger, the tendency of the law among jurisdictions to prohibit such extreme measures is steadily growing. Even in those jurisdictions in which the statutes and court cases continue to permit deadly force to be used to prevent felonies in which life is not endangered police departments are prohibiting it through their policies and regulations.

Once a crime has been committed, the chief law enforcement interest is the apprehension of the offender. Although laws vary, deadly force may generally be used to effect the arrest of a dangerous criminal who is endangering or has threatened human life, but this amount of force may not be used on a thief no matter how much he stole. No jurisdiction punishes theft with the death penalty, so no officer should apply "capital punishment" to a thief.

In no jurisdiction is deadly force permitted to effect an arrest for a misdemeanor. If the subject resists, the officer may escalate the amount of his force until it becomes deadly, it this is necessary to protect himself from death or great bodily injury, and the officer is not required to retreat. However, the use of deadly force is not justified to apprehend a misdemeanant even though he is in flight and there is no other way to capture him.

The right of self-defense is based on the necessity of permitting a person who is attacked to take reasonable steps to prevent harm to himself. This right permits him to use any reasonable force to prevent threatened harm, offensive bodily contact, or confinement. Since it is a defense to a charge or accusation of use of force, the burden is on the actor to show the facts which caused him to use force and that it was reasonable.

The privilege to act to defend oneself arises not only when the danger is real but even when the danger does not in fact exist, providing that the belief in the presence and degree of anger is reasonable. For example, if after a long, high speed, wild and reckless attempt on the part of a motorist to escape an officer the offender stops, leaps from his car and whips his hand inside his jacket, it would be reasonable for the officer to believe that he was about to be fired upon. It would be lawful use of deadly force for the officer to draw and fire his sidearm at the offender even if, in fact, the motorist was unarmed and reaching for only his wallet and driver license. The belief that he is threatened, however, must be that which a reasonable man would have under the circumstances. The person defending himself is not required to restrain himself with outstanding bravery, but on the other hand the reasonable man standard does not permit an abject coward to attack when there is no reasonable ground for his belief that he is in danger.

If force is continued after at attacker is disarmed, defeated, helpless, or the danger has passed, it is unlawful. No matter how gross he provocation had been on the part of the original attacker, there is no right to continue the use of force for revenge or punishment.

No officer should possess or use any weapon or incapacitating device which is neither issued nor approved by his department, including the ammunition in his firearm. Naturally, issued or approved weapons which have been materially altered to increase the force which they may apply should also not be possessed or used.

Under normal circumstances only the methods or weapons listed below should be used to apply force. It is the officer's responsibility to first exhaust every reasonable means of employing lesser force before escalating to a more severe application of force. The following methods are listed in ascending order from the least severe to the most drastic:

1. Physical strength and skill
2. Approved noxious substance, mace, gas, etc.
3. Approved baton, sap, or blackjack
4. Approved sidearm or other firearm loaded with approved ammunition.

Weapons should never be brandished or displayed as a threat unless their use under the circumstances would be reasonable and lawful.

Only those security devices or measures issued or approved by the department should be used to restrain those in custody, and the devices and measures should be used reasonably and only for the purpose of preventing:

1. Escape
2. Destruction of evidence
3. Attack
4. Self-inflicted injury
5. Commission of an offense

An officer who, out of anger or for the purpose of inflicting punishment or pain, cinches handcuffs too tightly, places a person in a straight jacket, strips a prisoner naked, puts an offender into a padded cell, incarcerates an offender with others who may attack him, or continues security measures when they are no longer reasonably necessary is acting unlawfully and reprehensibly. It is the responsibility of the courts to punish, not the police.

The decision of an officer to use handcuffs or not is a difficult one. Opinions on this subject vary among experienced, professional officers. Where departmental regulations have been issued which state the circumstances under which handcuffs shall, may, or must not be utilized they should be followed. However, because of the difficulty involved in covering all the possible situations in a regulation, they have not been written for officers' guidance in many agencies. The officer must then utilize his professional discretion.

The officer who decides whether or not to use handcuffs on the basis of his answer to, "If I were this prisoner, would I realize or could I be lead to understand that handcuffs are reasonable and necessary?" will arrive at the appropriate conclusion. An officer who states that "I handcuff everybody I arrest," does not, it is to be hoped, really do so. It is obviously ridiculous to handcuff "little old ladies" and small children without exception. On the other hand, the officer who fails to restrain dangerous felons, persons in a state of rage, or others who can be reasonably expected to do any of the acts which security measures are designed to prevent certainly should be handcuffed.

An officer who fails to use his cuffs when it is appropriate endangers himself, his coworkers, the prisoner, and others. Persons who are restrained by security devices are helpless, and officers must remain constantly aware of the possibility that such prisoners may be injured or suffer needlessly if precautions are not utilized. Therefore, secured persons must not be left unattended unnecessarily or otherwise subjected to needless danger or discomfort. The variety of possible situations to be avoided are too numerous to mention, but two must be. Prisoners should never be handcuffed to a vehicle which is used to transport them. If the vehicle is involved in an accident, they cannot be removed from it if the officer is incapacitated or otherwise incapable of releasing them. It is appropriate to restrain handcuffed prisoners with safety belts because anyone can release the belts. However, if the person is handcuffed to the vehicle, only an officer can provide the key to the cuffs. Prisoners who indicate that they need to relieve themselves must be permitted to do so as soon as possible. The officer who refuses to permit his prisoner to use toilet facilities or to aid the nauseated person who must vomit is inflicting cruel and unusual punishment upon him.

Search and Seizure

The most important factor relating to the law of search and seizure, and what each officer should seriously consider before he begins any search for or collection of evidence is that WHENEVER POSSIBLE A SEARCH WARRANT SHOULD BE OBTAINED BEFORE SEARCHING FOR OR SEIZING EVIDENCE.

Both state and federal constitutions guarantee to everybody protection against unreasonable searches and seizures. This protection extends to their person, houses, papers, and other property. No search warrant may be issued without probable cause, supported by oath or affirmation, and every warrant must particularly describe the place to be searched and the persons or things to be seized.

The protection given by the Fourth Amendment arose from the unpleasant experiences suffered by colonial Americans when searches by English soldiers were conducted under the authority of "writs of assistance" or "general warrants." These writs and warrants were issued with little restraint, without probable cause, and empowered authorities to conduct searches virtually any place on the mere suspicion that goods subject to seizure might be discovered.

The words of the Fourth Amendment must be interpreted by the courts so that the meaning of the law can be applied to the fact situations of each case presented. Thousands of cases have defined "person," "houses," "probable cause," "search," and other words which appear in the Amendment.

Although persons subjected to unlawful searches and seizures have recourse to civil actions against officials who violate their rights, the most common procedure by which they protect themselves is through the application of the exclusionary evidence rule. The exclusionary rule is simply that evidence obtained by unreasonable searches and seizures will not be admitted upon trial, usually upon objection raised by the defendant at a pre-trial "suppression hearing." The rule is not provided for in the Constitution, rather it was developed by the courts as their solution to the means by which the provision of the Amendment would be enforced, not adopt it. Today, however, it is universally applied in both federal and state courts because of the holding of the Supreme Court of the United States in the case of Mapp v. Ohio in 1961. The purpose to be fulfilled by the rule is that officers will be deterred from illegally searching for or seizing evidence when they know that it cannot be used against the defendant to prove his guilt.

Search Warrants

A search warrant is an order written in the name of the State, signed by a judicial officer in the proper exercise of his authority, directing a sheriff, constable, or other officer to search a specified place for evidence, stolen property or other "fruits" of a crime, or contraband, and to bring the articles enumerated before the court if they are discovered.

The following are criteria or requirements which must be met before a valid search warrant may be issued:

1. **Probable Cause**

    If the facts in the affidavit are sufficient to lead a reasonable and prudent man to believe that a crime has been committed and that the articles described can be found at the place specified, then issuance of a search warrant is justified. Information received by an officer from an undisclosed informant may be used as the basis for a search warrant, but the applicant for the warrant must be able to give the judicial officer substantial reasons to support the probable validity of the information which has been provided. The underlying circumstances upon which the applicant bases his belief must be specified by him. It is not sufficient to merely state, even with fervor, the police officer's belief. The facts of which he is aware which led to the development of that belief must also be stated.

2. **Oath of Affirmation**

    If this requirement is not fulfilled, the evidence obtained will not be admitted. The presumption that the magistrate had sworn the applicant is rebuttable by the defendant, and if no oath was administered the warrant is invalid and the evidence will be lost (excluded).

3. **Particular Description of Place and Things**

    Whatever the wording to describe the place to be searched, the objective to be served is that the officers who are commanded to conduct the search will not, if they follow the description included in the warrant, search the wrong premises and disturb the rights of the innocent. If the warrant does not identify the property to be seized, it will not justify any seizure of that property. Contraband such as prohibited arms, explosive devices, and gambling equipment will ordinarily not be required to be as specifically described as stolen goods, since contraband is sizeable by any officer lawfully observing it. When warrants are obtained for contraband, the best description possible under the circumstances should always be attempted.

4. **Issuing Official**

    The purpose served by requiring warrants is to assure that the innocent will not be disturbed by uncontrolled and unreasonable actions of officials of the executive branch of government. Therefore, the impartial and objective consideration by the judiciary of the probable cause and the reasonableness of the contemplated action is interposed as a restraint. Attempts to bypass this objective, even to accomplish other well-founded purposes such as the efficient issuance of warrants, have generally been found unconstitutional by the courts.

5. **Property Subject to Seizure**

Under early law, only stolen property could be seized under a search warrant. However, types of articles subject to seizure have been greatly expanded. Limitations still exist in some states such as requiring that only stolen or embezzled property (fruits of the crime), articles used to commit the crime (instrumentalities), or articles which are prohibited or controlled by statutes (contraband) may be seized. Such restrictions prevent officers from taking objects which are important as evidence, such as shoes worn by a suspect which could be compared with footprints found at the scene, but which fail to meet the definition of statutory restrictions. The United States Supreme Court in *Warden v. Hoyden* held in 1967, that statutes which permitted search warrants to issue for "mere evidence" are constitutional. It is up to those states which still follow the old rule to change their statutes or court decisions to permit seizure of evidence, but they are not required to do so.

Only those items specified in the warrant may be seized. If other property is seized, it must be under authority other than that provided by the warrant.

6. **Execution Only By Those Ordered**

A search warrant may only be executed by those commanded by it to act, but the person designated may be specifically by either name or class (peace officers, for example). The person designated may be assisted by others, however.

7, **Time Limit**

A search warrant must be executed within a reasonable time or it will fail to meet constitutional requirements. The amount of time which is reasonable varies, of course, according to the circumstances of each case. Most jurisdictions have by statute limited the time in which a search warrant may be executed, and the permissible period varies from a number of hours to more than a week. Some jurisdictions require special judicial authorization for warrants to be served at night

8. **Prior Notice, Demand, and Forcible Entry**

If the local law allows and the warrant is for the seizure of items which can be destroyed quickly or if officers are aware of facts which reasonably lead them to believe notice to occupants would lead to danger of attack, entry may usually be effected without notice. Otherwise they are first required to notify persons within the premises of their identity and right to enter and make a demand that they be permitted to enter. Reasonable and necessary force may be used to effect entry when officers must act quickly to avoid evidence destruction or attack, or if they are denied entry after notice has been given and their demand had been refused. Force may also be used to enter unoccupied premises or when the denial is passive, for example, when occupants remain silent and do not open the door.

Warrantless Searches and Seizures

Three factors have influenced and caused the development of those laws under which warrantless searches are permitted. They are permitted and lawful:

1. By consent
2. When necessity or emergency require immediate action
3. Where no right to protection exists

Consent Searches

A general principle of law is that one can waive any right or privilege to which he is entitled. However, because rights and privileges have arisen from previously experienced problems, court observe very carefully the evidence presented in support of contentions that a defendant consented to a search.

Consent must be voluntary, the prosecution has the burden of proving consent clearly, and some sort of positive action by the person waiving must be shown. For example, unless the person positively states his consent or makes some clearly understood gesture, the consent will not be held to be voluntary.

The search cannot extend beyond that granted by the terms of the consent in either area or time. That is, consent to search a room will not permit other rooms or the whole house to be searched, and the person may stop the search at any time simply by revoking his consent.

The person consenting must have the capacity to do so. A person who has the right to possess premises or things may give consent, but others may not. For example, the occupant of a hotel room may consent to its search but not the management, a parent can consent to a search of a minor child's room but not that of an adult child if the room is exclusively that child's, although permission to search areas used in common by the family is valid; a minor child's consent is unlikely to be held valid, but an adult child can consent to a search of at least jointly used areas; a spouse can consent if the premises are occupied by both spouses; and a person caring for the personal property of another may permit search of it.

Immediate Action Required

The most prevalent situations under which this exception is granted are searches made incident to a lawful arrest. Necessity is the motivating factor in permitting these searches. The two purposes served are to protect the arresting officer from attack and to prevent the person from access to things which would facilitate his escape, and to assure that evidence will not be destroyed by the defendant.

Should any of the following criteria not be met, the evidence discovered will be excluded:

1. The arrest must be lawful.
2. The search must be made for the purposes listed above (protection, security, evidence).
   An arrest for an unlicensed vehicle, to be followed by a citation, may not be the basis for a search for drugs as there is no relationship between the offense and the purpose of the search.
3. The arrest must not be a sham or subterfuge made only to initiate a search not based on reasonable cause.

An arrest warrant sworn out by officers (who merely suspect a burglary by the subject) charging the defendant with spitting on the sidewalk for the purpose of gaining entrance to his residence when they execute it, evidence of the burglary would be excluded.

Both the area searched and the time during which the search will be permitted are limited. Officers may make a reasonable search of areas within the person's reach or the distance through which he might be able to quickly leap in order to obtain a weapon for attack or evidence to destroy. Searching for evidence during an arrest beyond this area is no longer permitted without a search warrant. The search must be made contemporaneously with the arrest. After the subject has been removed from the scene and/or confined in jail, the necessity of immediate action no longer prevails, and the officer must obtain a search warrant to search the area of the arrest. An arrested person may be immediately fully searched, as opposed to a mere pat-down for weapons, incident to an arrest for which he is actually being taken into custody, or the search may be delayed until booking.

Once in jail, an arrestee or his property room effects may be researched without a warrant where the searches are not unreasonably made, i.e., harassment searches.

The right of officers to search a car beyond the reach of the subject being arrested, for example in the closed trunk or even the locked glove compartment,, would have to be based on grounds other than the arrest itself, i.e., on probable cause to search those areas, on consent, or "plain sight," or on a valid inventory.

When probable cause exists and the evidence is contained within a moving (or about to be moved) vehicle, officers may search. There is a significant difference in the necessity for immediate action between searches of buildings and searches of vehicles which may speedily be moved out of the jurisdiction before a search warrant can be obtained. An occupied car on a highway is movable, and the persons within it are alerted to the presence of officers. The evidence may never again be located if courts were to require officers to obtain a warrant to search under these circumstances. To conduct a warrantless search of a "moving" vehicle, the officer should have that amount of information which would cause a court to readily issue a search warrant if there were time to procure one. The officer may make the search without first arresting the person. The search will be upheld under the vehicle exception if the essential requirements of probable cause are shown to have existed prior to the search.

Where No Right to Protection Exists

Seizures of evidence without a search is not a violation of the Fourth Amendment when officers are lawfully present and the article seized is seen by them. Courts do not require officers to leave obvious evidence to be destroyed, but officers must not be trespassers at the time the evidence is observed. Furthermore, if an officer is a trespasser when he does see evidence, he cannot then procure a search warrant on the basis of the information he acquired as a trespasser.

The protection offered by constitutional provisions are to protect persons against the acts of government officers, not private parties. Therefore, if a private person obtains evidence through unlawful entrance or burglary, the evidence may be used against the criminal defendant. Of course, if an officer initiated the private person's action or participated in it, the evidence would be excluded. Searches and seizures are unlawful when they reasonably intrude into areas where the person can reasonably expect privacy, but not outside those areas. Open fields, public streets, and other places of similar description are outside the restrictions of the Fourth Amendment.

Inventories of vehicles which come into the hand of the police through impounding procedures are permitted. The inventory made of the vehicle is for the purpose of making an inventory of its contents to protect the owner rather than a search for evidence of an offense. The officer's intrusion is only justifiable if it is a good faith attempt to protect the property in the car. In effect, the evidence is discovered "accidentally" while the officer is doing what he has a right to do and where he has legitimate cause to be.

POLICE SCIENCE NOTES

POLICIES, PROCEDURES, AND REGULATIONS

Good, effective management techniques applied to any organization require that each person within the agency knows what is expected of him and what to expect of others as they carry out their functions and bring the group effort to life. Professional management is important to police departments, too. All officers and employees should be well informed as to what they are to do, how they are to do it, and the goals to be attained by both their own unit and the department as a whole.

Every person in the organization should know exactly the person who is his superior as well as those who are his subordinates.

Channels should be established through which information flows up and down and through which authority is delegated. These lines of control permit the delegation of authority, the placing of responsibility, the supervision of work, and the coordination of effort. Lines of control should be clearly defined and well understood by all members so that each may know to whom he is responsible and who, in turn, is responsible to him.

Sound and adequate enforcement policies are essential to gaining enforcement objectives and will guide police officers in putting into effect the kind of enforcement program envisioned by the administration. Clear statements of policy will help to resolve doubts in determining administrative intent. Policy development is essential to the success of any organization, and policies should be in writing so that they can be used as the basis on which the departmental operations are constructed.

Policy indicates the general course of direction of an organization, within which the activities of the personnel and units must operate. This establishment of *general* administrative guidelines relates to and complements the main objectives of the organization. For example, the policy concerning the issuance of citations in traffic accident cases might take the following form: "Violations of driving regulations cause traffic accidents, and accidents may be reduced to effective traffic law enforcement. Violators should be issued citations when evidence exists to justify such action." The intent of this policy statement is to inform officers that the policy of the department is to enforce laws. Obviously, this policy is not concerned with the procedures to be followed in preparing each citation, nor does it establish any precise rules. Procedures and rules and regulations must not only follow policy, but must originate from policy.

Established policy, although allowing individual supervisors to think for themselves, limits possible mistakes within manageable bounds. Independent thinking should be encouraged because it develops administrative abilities. Potential executives can be developed only by permitting discretion and initiative on the part of the supervisors. Carefully delineated policy statements allow this latitude.

The term *Policy* is not synonymous with *Procedure*, nor do either of these terms have the same meaning as *Rules and Regulations*. The following definitions are offered to clarify and insure uniformity of terminology:

Policy

Policy consists of principles and values which guide the performance of a department in a particular situation. It is a statement of guiding principles which should be followed in activities which are directed toward the attainment of department objectives. Policy is formulated by analyzing objectives and determining through research those principles which will best guide the department in achieving its objectives. Policy is based upon police ethics and experience, the desires of the community and the mandate of the law.

Policy is articulated to inform the public and department employees of the principles which will be adhered to in the performance of the law enforcement function. Additionally, policy establishes operational standards to assist department employees in the necessary exercise of discretion in discharging their responsibility.

An officer in the performance of his duty is confronted with an infinite variety of complex situations which require police action. Since policy is objective rather than situation oriented, it is broad enough in scope to encompass most situations. Policy, therefore, must be stated in general terms.

Procedure

A procedure is a method of performing an operation or a manner of proceeding on a course of action. It differs from policy in that it directs action in a particular situation to perform a specific task within the guidelines of policy. Both policies and procedures are objective oriented; however, policy establishes limits of action while procedure directs response within those limits.

Rule or Regulation

A rule or regulation is a specific prohibition or requirement which is stated to prevent deviations from policy or procedure. Rules and regulations allow little deviation other than for stated exceptions.

Many departments have been studied by police management consultants, and the results of these surveys are, with few exceptions, predictable. The larger the agency, the better their policies and procedures and the greater the change that they are all in writing and periodically reviewed and changed to fit present circumstances.

Policy and procedure formulation require planning and research. The larger agencies can afford such activities but the smaller ones cannot. The larger the organization is the greater likelihood that there is a formalized planning and research unit with permanent staff personnel.

Of the nearly 40,000 police departments in the United States, 98.9% have less than 100 personnel, and 82.2% have less than five.

There should be written directives applicable to auxiliary officers. At the very minimum these should cover such matters as eligibility for membership, application procedures, use of equipment and the wearing of the uniform, agency organization, disciplinary procedures, powers of arrest, use of force (including carrying of weapons both on and off duty), pursuit driving restrictions, and procedures for separation from the force.

Sworn officers are administered oaths before entering upon their duties. The intention is to impress upon officers that their conduct must be exemplary. Oaths of office for the police and codes of ethics are usually brief, but their every word is of the greatest import.

The departmental oath for auxiliary police may be included in the application for membership in the auxiliary police. The following oath is typical:

> I hereby acknowledge my complete understanding that the standby law enforcement assignment for which I am volunteering carries with it the requirement that I will, without question, obey and execute to the best of my ability the legal orders of those designated to supervise and command my activities; that I am to complete all assigned training courses; and that my violation or disregard of the Rules and Regulations of my organization will be cause for disciplinary action or dismissal. Furthermore, I understand that any false statements intentionally made in my application disqualifies me for membership in the _____ Police Auxiliary.
> Signed:_____
> Date:_____

The community expects better and more moral behavior from the police than they do of both over governmental employees and members of the private sector. These expectations apply both on and off duty, and all officers are subjected to close scrutiny in all their statements and actions. The community demands that those who enforce group standards rigidly abide by them.

Following are basic principles guiding conduct applicable to the police:

Courtesy

Officers are expected to be courteous at all times no matter how great the provocation, even if such would cause others to lose their tempers. This is not to say that they are to be servile. Although it is true that they are servants of the public need, they are not servants of individual members of the community as officers act within their sphere of authority. It is not difficult to be courteous when one learns to be an *objective* enforcer of the law, and this means that personal prejudices and animosities are to be repressed. Officers should be particularly attentive to persons who seek information or assistance and in each case try to put themselves in the "others' shoes"—no officer should act toward persons in any manner other than what he would reasonably expect from them under similar circumstances. It must be constantly borne in mind by policemen that many persons whom they will meet professionally will be under great stress and may act in ways that they will later regret. But the officer who acts unprofessionally will be remembered negatively. The person who provoked the officer will then blame the officer for all that transpired, and the lawbreaker will then have a "patsy" on which to blame his own faults.

Punctuality

Officers should be punctual in their engagements and expeditious in the performance of their duties. Again, the community expects more from them than from others.

Professional Objectivity

The professional officer is just, impartial, and reasonable in his enforcement of the laws he is sworn to uphold. Objective law enforcement never includes overstepping the limits of legal authority and power, and the officer's action or inaction will never be for personal gain or in vengeance.

Protection of Public Funds

Officers are custodians of the public property entrusted to their care and shall not misuse their equipment or otherwise be wasteful of public funds.

Cooperation

Law enforcement is a cooperative effort among the community and other governmental agencies. Full cooperation by policemen should be offered to both private and public groups so that the safety and welfare of the community will be assured.

Communication

The professional officer actively disseminates practical and useful information to others regarding matters of the public safety and welfare. He does not passively wait for others to come to him.

Exemplary Conduct

The professional officer's conduct, both public and private, is such that the public regards him as an example of fidelity, stability and morality.

Governmental Allegiance

Officers should be faithful in the allegiance to our government, loyal to the ethics of their profession, and accept as a sacred obligation their responsibility as citizens to support the

Constitutions of the Nation and their State and to defend our principles of liberty. Departmental rules, violation of which subjects the member to disciplinary action, often include the following:

Respect, Language

Active lack of respect, manifested by abusive language or non-verbal communication directed toward other personnel or members of the public, is prohibited.

Disobedience

The violation of or deliberate delay in the prompt completion of activities directed to be performed by the lawful orders of any superior officer is prohibited.

Confidentiality

Divulgence of any information concerning the plans, actions, internal activities or case materials of the police department without authority is prohibited.

Intoxication

The use at any time of any intoxicating drug or material proscribed by law is prohibited, and reporting for duty while under the influence of the consumption of any intoxicant while on duty is prohibited, although the ingestion of intoxicants necessarily required by the nature of the assigned (usually undercover) duties being performed by the officer may be permitted.

Misconduct

Any breach of the peace, neglect of duty, or misconduct either within or without the jurisdiction which tends to subvert the good order, efficiency, or discipline of the department or the auxiliary force or which reflects discredit upon the department is prohibited.

Misuse of Position

Affiliation with any group which professes to represent the police department or other agency of the criminal justice system while purporting to act as a representative of the police agency, and utilizing or making reference to one's affiliation with the department to sway others for political purposes is prohibited without lawful permission of superiors of the department for professional purpose.

Wearing of Uniform and Use of Equipment

The auxiliary police will wear only prescribed or issued uniform items, utilize only prescribed or issued equipment or weapons, and maintain these items; and any officer failing to meet these requirements shall be subject to disciplinary action.

Off-Duty Weapons

Off-duty auxiliary officers shall neither carry nor utilize any weapon in contravention to the laws applicable to citizens not falling within the statutory exemptions concerning the possession or use of weapons (or, for those agencies which permit by regulation the carrying of off-duty weapons). Off-duty auxiliary officers may carry any weapon permitted by law upon prior approval by and registration with the department.

Any action by an auxiliary police officer that is illegal or contrary to departmental rules and regulations subjects that officer to disciplinary action, including separation from the force.

POLICE SCIENCE NOTES
INTERVIEWS, INTERROGATION, AND RULES OF EVIDENCE

INTRODUCTION

Making investigations is a very important part of any peace officer's daily work. In the early stages of an investigation, facts often may appear to be crystal clear. The whole picture may change, however, after a thorough investigation is made. A serious crime may be disclosed. An incident, on the other hand, may appear to be very serious but, in reality, it turns out to be a minor occurrence. The peace officer's job is to investigate and get the facts.

Authorities are pretty much in agreement that more than 85 percent of police investigative time is expended in talking to people. More surprising than that, to most people, is the fact that more than 99 percent of all evidence offered during the trial of a case is oral testimony—what witnesses say under oath.

Obviously, then, an investigator must know how to get information from people and how to evaluate it. He must know something about the art of conducting an interview or an interrogation to do that. But skill in conducting an interview or an interrogation can never supplant the need to make a good investigation. A good investigation is the essence of effective police work.

Sometimes a peace officer may fail to recognize, moreover, that more than technical skills are needed if he is to discharge his duties effectively and intelligently. He must be alert at all times during the course of any investigation, whether it is a minor traffic accident or the brutal killing of another human being, to secure evidence (facts) that will be admissible in a criminal court. A working knowledge of the rules of evidence is a necessity for all law enforcement officers.

It often has been said that criminal cases are won or lost at the scene of the offense. Police officers are aware that accurate and thorough investigation is the foundation of successful prosecution. But not always are they aware that something more than sound investigation is required in order to support their case. Court dockets reveal that countless cases have been lost because some important bit of evidence laboriously collected and relied upon by the police officer to establish the case, has been thrown out because it did not satisfy the rules of evidence. Evidence must be obtained which will be admissible in court. The officer *must* understand the fundamental rules governing the admission and rejection of evidence. These are the rules which shed light on the apparent mysteries and obscurities of trial procedures and make it possible for the officer to prepare a case which will enable judge and jury to receive reliable information upon which to base a proper decision.

INTERVIEWS AND INTERROGATION

Importance of the Subject Matter

The interviewing of witnesses and prospective informants, and the interrogation of criminal suspects, are the investigative methods most frequently used by the police. In fact, most of our serious crimes would remain unsolved if it were not for investigative leads and the proof of guilt that result from the use of these procedures. A well-designed course in police interviews and interrogations makes provision for 30 or more hours of instruction. Only the most important techniques can be considered in this lesson.

Basic Definitions

(1) To interview means to ask questions for the purpose of securing information. However, when the word "interview" is used, there is an implication that the desired information will be voluntarily given. (2) To interrogate also means to ask questions. But, when the word "interrogate" is used, there is an implication that the investigator's request for information will be met with resistance by the subject.

"Interrogate," as used in police work, includes the entire contact of the officer with the subject. Reactions, time lapses, attitude, emotional response, and many other factors may be just as important to an officer as the words used by the subject.

For the balance of this lesson, the words "interview" and "interrogation" may be used interchangeably. Both situations involve conversation with a purpose. The fundamental principles apply in either case.

Basic Rule

NO ONE IS LEGALLY OBLIGED, AS A GENERAL STATEMENT, TO PROVIDE INFORMATION FOR THE POLICE. There are exceptions to this rule, but they are few. Parties involved in certain vehicular accidents must make reports to the proper police authorities. Operators of motor vehicles must furnish the police certain information when a demand is made for it. There are other circumstances in which the police must be given information. But, generally, in regard to the subject of a police interrogation, the basic rule is correct. Police officers must rely upon skill in obtaining information from people.

Most interrogation efforts must be directed at making the subject want to provide the needed information. The art, or science (caE it what you will) of interrogation, is measured by the ability of the interrogator to bring the subject to the point where he chooses to be of assistance.

Warning of Rights
The U.S. Supreme Court in the case of *Miranda v. Arizona* held that it was unconstitutional for officers to interrogate a person in custody without first warning him of his right. Before questioning a suspect who is detained, then, an officer must first inform him that:

1. He has a right to remain silent
2. Any statement he does make will be used as evidence against him
3. He has the right to the presence of an attorney
4. If he cannot afford an attorney one shall be retained or appointed for him

Enforcement of this rule is through the operation of the *exclusionary evidence rule*. If it is shown that the defendant did not receive the proper warning before questioning, all confessions, statements, admissions, and any other evidence discovered because of what he has said will not be permitted into evidence. Every officer should have in his immediate possession a card issued by his department or the prosecutor on which the necessary warnings are printed. He should read those warnings *word for word* before he begins any questioning of a suspect.

All confessions are not excluded if warnings are not first given. The court's interest is in protecting persons against being compelled by police to give statements through questioning. Therefore, it is not applied where a private person questions the suspect (unless the private person is acting for the police) or the suspect blurts out his confession on his own without being questioned.

As with nearly all rights, the rights to silence and the presence of an attorney may be waived by the suspect. However, the waiver must be made voluntarily, knowingly, and intelligently. Courts are faced daily with the difficult decision of determining whether the defendant or the officer is telling the truth about a waiver of rights. Therefore, as much as is possible the officer should obtain a *signed* waiver of rights before he begins his questioning. Every police department should have such forms printed and immediately available to all officers.

Even where a suspect has waived his right to silence, etc., and/or has made statements if at any time he indicates that he no longer wishes to talk or wishes an attorney, questioning must stop immediately.

Involuntary confessions, statements, or admissions will also be exclude from evidence. Involuntariness is induced by: promises, hopes of reward, or benefit; or coercion through violence, fear, or threats.

Privacy

The principal psychological factor contributing to successful interrogation is privacy—being alone with the person under interrogation. This we all seem to realize instinctively in our own private or social affairs, but in criminal interrogations it is generally overlooked or ignored. For instance, in asking a personal friend or acquaintance to divulge a secret, we carefully avoid making the request in the presence of other persons; we seek a time and place when the matter can be discussed in private. Likewise, when anyone harbors a troublesome problem that he would like to "get off his chest," he finds it easier to confide in another person alone rather than in the presence of a third person. This is so even though the other person may also be one to whom the disturbed individual would like to reveal the same information. In other words, if B and C are equally good friends of A, and A wants to discuss his troubles with both B and C, it will be easier for A to first talk to one of them alone, for example, to B, and then, on another occasion, to make the same disclosure to the other one. A moment's reflection by anyone upon his own past experiences will readily satisfy him regarding the privacy requirements for confidential or embarrassing disclosures. Nevertheless, in criminal interrogations, where the same mental processes are in operation, and to an even greater degree by reason of the criminality of the disclosure, interrogators generally seem to lose sight of the fact that a suspect or witness is much more apt to reveal his secrets in the privacy of a room occupied by himself and his interrogator than in the presence of an additional person or persons.

In the famous Degnan murder case in Chicago (1945-46), the importance of privacy was impressively revealed by the murderer himself. William Heirens, a 17-year-old college student, was accused of the brutal killing of 6-year-old Suzanne Degnan. His fingerprints were found on a ransom note left in the Degnan home and the handwriting on the note was identified as his. There was also evidence that he had killed two other persons and committee 29 burglaries. His attorneys, to whom he apparently admitted his guilt, advised him to confess to the prosecuting attorney and therefore afford them an opportunity to save him from the electric chair.

Arrangements were made, by Heirens' counsel, with the Cook County State's attorney to take Heirens' confession, but at the appointed time and place Heirens refused to confess. The reason for this last-minute refusal appears in the following headline from the Chicago Daily News of August 2, 1946: "Youth asks Privacy at Conference. Blames Refusal to Talk on Large Crowd at Parley." The newspaper account further stated: "It was learned that Heirens balked at a conference arranged for last Tuesday because (the Prosecuting attorney) had invited almost 30 law enforcement officers and others to be present. It was at the conference between the youth and his lawyers that he told them for the first time that there were "too many" present on Tuesday. He said he would go through the confession arrangements to escape the electric chair if it could be done under different conditions. The State's attorney told reporters that he had invited the police officials to the conference because they had all played a leading part in the investigation and he felt they should be "in on the finish."

Another Chicago newspaper, the Chicago Times of August 2, 1946, reported: "It was hinted the original confession program was a flop because the youth was frightened by the movie-like setting in (the State's attorney's) office. Presumably he was frightened out of memory, too. 'I don't remember.' His self-consciousness reportedly was deepened by the presence of several members of the police department, especially (the police officer) whose handiness with flower pots as weapons brought about Heirens' expose in a burglary attempt.
"At the second setting for the taking of Heirens' confession, the number of spectators was reduced by about half, but a reading of the confession gives the impression that Heirens, though admitting his guilt, withheld—for understandable reasons—about 50 percent of the gruesome details and true explanations of his various crimes."
"It is indeed a said commentary upon police interrogation practices when a 17-year-old boy has to impart an elementary lesson to top-ranking law enforcement officials, i.e., that it is psychologically unsound to ask a person to confess a crime in the presence of 30 spectators."

Reports and How To Ask Questions

Another cardinal rule of interrogation is "never to solicit or accept information without making it a matter of record." If you accept information, you also accept responsibility. That does not mean, however, that each time a question is asked of a person that the response must be reduced to writing. The rule is construed to apply to investigative situations. In such a situation, as a matter of self-protection and as a guarantee that you fulfill your obligation, such information should be reduced to writing and made a matter of record.

Finally, in questioning a witness make use of the following basic interrogatories: (1) when, (2) where, (3) who, (4) what, (5) how, and (6) why. Another good interrogatory to use that can be quite fruitful is: Why not? By asking those questions, or as many of them as are applicable, enough information can be obtained to prepare a good report.

THE RULES OF EVIDENCE

Evidence Defined and Described

Evidence is defined as that which tends to prove or disprove any matter or to influence the belief respecting it. It is further defined in legal acceptation and as including *all the means* by which any alleged matter of fact, the truth of which is submitted for investigation, is established or disproved. Although the term "evidence" is sometimes used interchangeably with the term "proof," there is substantial distinction between the two.

Evidence and Proof Distinguished

The word "proof" as used in the law of evidence is an ambiguous word. "Proof" is the end result of conviction or persuasion produced by evidence. Put another way, "proof is only the effect or result of evidence, and evidence is only the medium of proof. In sum, then, evidence plus evidence plus evidence equals proof.

The Nature of the Law of Evidence

The law of evidence relates to the use of evidence before judicial tribunals, and, in its proper significance, consists of: (1) certain rules as to the exclusion of evidence, and (2) the rules which prescribe the manner of presenting evidence in the courts.

How Evidence is Brought Out

Evidence is adduced in a courtroom by: (1) oral testimony, (2) real evidence, and (3) writings. Writings, as used in the law of evidence, is a broad term that includes documents, affidavits, and depositions, and court records.

Evidence Classified

The term "evidence" is an exceptionally broad one—so broad, in fact, that three major classifications are now recognized: *direct* evidence, *circumstantial* evidence, and *real* evidence.

Direct evidence is that means of proof which tends to show the existence of a fact in question without the intervention of the proof of any other fact. It is evidence that is based on the personal knowledge of a witness which came to him by means of one of his five senses.

Donigan and Fisher, in their book, pages 3-5, distinguish the three major classes of evidence in the following way: If a man takes the stand and says: "I saw Joe Doake draw a gun and fire twice into the body of this man who fell over," that is direct evidence. It is direct because an eyewitness is describing what he saw—facts which he knows of his own knowledge obtained by means of one of his five senses.

But suppose that a witness testifies: "Joe Doake and John Smith went into a clothes closet together. The door closed behind them. There were no windows, airways, or other means of ingress or egress. Nobody entered or left. The closet was empty before Doake and Smith went in. Suddenly I heard a shot. Doake rushed out of the closet with a smoking gun in his hand. I rushed into the closet and found Smith lying on the floor. He had been shot in the back, behind the shoulder blades."

That is *circumstantial* evidence as to who killed Smith. The man on the witness stand did not see Doake fire the fatal shot, and yet these facts as related by the witness are so closely associated with the fact at issue (who killed Smith) that the killing may be reasonably inferred therefrom. Thus, direct and circumstantial evidence can be easily distinguished. Direct evidence is testimony relating the immediate experience on the part of a witness. The essence of circumstantial evidence is logical inference. The existence of the principal fact is inferred from one or more circumstances which have been established directly.

Real evidence is simply physical evidence—evidence furnished by things themselves, on view or inspection. It is evidence which speaks for itself and requires no explanation, merely identification. Such evidence is extremely important, not only because of its effect on the jury but because of the range of subjects covered. There have been cases in which the aroma of whiskey and the music from an aria were admitted as real evidence. Photographs, moving pictures, x-rays, maps, diagrams, experiments and tests conducted in court, views of premises, exhibitions of the person—all are real evidence

Admissibility of Evidence

Before any evidence can be admitted in a court, it must meet three tests. Evidence must be: (1) relevant, (2) material, and (3) competent. In some situations, evidence will be excluded even though it meets the three general tests. The three general tests of admissibility are supplemented by other rules which for the most part simply provide different ways of trying to promote a fair and impartial trial. For example, courts usually will reject evidence that is unduly prejudicial. Evidence that a defendant has been convicted of other crimes is rejected except under certain circumstances as being unduly prejudicial. Many more examples could be given when evidence would be excluded through relevant, material, and competent.

Special Rules of Evidence

There are no universal rules of evidence. Rulings of courts may vary from one state to another. Common law rules still exist in some states, but have been modified by statute in others, and to an increasing extent, the rules of evidence are being codified by legislative enactments. Every police officer should be acquainted with the evidentiary rules of his particular state.

The Hearsay Rule

Ask the man on the street what he knows about the law of evidence. Usually the only doctrine he will be able to mention is the one called by the old English word hearsay. In the law of evidence the word embraces what lawyers refer to as "The Hearsay Rule and Its Exceptions."

"Briefly, hearsay evidence is information relayed from one person to the witness before it reaches the ears of the court or jury. Its value, if any, is measured by the credibility to be given to some third person not sworn as a witness to the fact, and consequently not subject to cross examination." An ancient rule of evidence that is known as the *hearsay rule* forbids the use of *objectionable hearsay evidence* in judicial proceedings.

The "rule is simply that hearsay evidence is generally inadmissible in court—because such evidence *may not be trustworthy* or reliable and there is no way to test its trustworthiness or reliability by cross-examination of the witness who is on the stand." The hearsay rule applies not only to oral statements but to written communications as well.

The law has recognized that injustice might be done unless certain exceptions to the rule were permitted. Each of the exceptions is based on the principle that the evidence, though technically objectionable hearsay, nevertheless is considered trustworthy and reliable because of certain protective circumstances, and sometimes, that some special necessity exists for its introduction.

Police officers should be acquainted with a number of real exceptions to the hearsay rule. Four of the exceptions are of greater concern to police officers than the others. These are: (1) Admissions, (2) Confessions, (3) Dying declarations, and (4) Spontaneous declarations—the res gestae rule.

A great deal of independent study on your part will be necessary if you are to gain a fair understanding of the hearsay rule and what must be established in order to use objectionable hearsay as a real exception to that rule.

Opinion Evidence

Another important rule of evidence that should be known by any police officer is "The Opinion Rule." Next to the hearsay rule, this rule of evidence has given rise to more problems in the courts than any other rule of evidence.

Generally speaking, it may be said that opinion is the exclusive province of the jury, and that witnesses will not be allowed to invade such province. A witness is to testify to facts, so that the jury may form an opinion as to such facts and render its verdict accordingly. This rule of evidence has its origin in our common law system of proof which is exacting in its insistence upon the most reliable sources of information.

The theory of the courts in restricting a witness to stating facts is that the triers of fact, either judge or jury, are as able to draw the proper inferences and conclusions as the witness, in the average case; however, the exclusion of opinion evidence does not extend to cases in which the factfinders are not as able to draw conclusions as the witness. There are subjects upon which opinion evidence is admissible.

Opinion evidence may be divided into lay opinion and expert opinion. A great many words would be needed in order to give a reasonable explanation of the scope and application of these two sides of the opinion rule. This lesson is not the proper place to attempt to do that.

CONCLUSION

The aim of this lesson has been to furnish you with enough information about the two topics discussed to make you aware of their importance in law enforcement. Both topics are so broad that it has been only possible to touch them lightly. The instructor can suggest some reference material that may be used to explore either topic in greater depth and, if you can find the time to read some of it, you will find it not only informative but interesting as well.